Celtic Journeys

Celtic Journeys

A Traveler's Guide
to Ireland's Spiritual Legacy

STEVE AND LOIS RABEY

CITADEL PRESS
Kensington Publishing Corp.
www.kensingtonbooks.com

CITADEL PRESS books are published by

Kensington Publishing Corp.
850 Third Avenue
New York, NY 10022

All Kensington titles, imprints, and distributed lines are available at special quantity discounts for bulk purchases for sales promotions, premiums, fund raising, educational, or institutional use. Special book excerpts or customized printings can also be created to fit specific needs. For details, write or phone the office of the Kensington special sales manager: Kensington Publishing Corp., 850 Third Avenue, New York, NY 10022, attn: Special Sales Department, phone 1-800-221-2647.

ISBN 0-8065-2161-9

First printing May 2001

10 9 8 7 6 5 4 3 2 1

Printed in the United States of America

Cataloging data may be obtained from the Library of Congress.

CONTENTS

Introduction   vii

PART I: THE SITES

1. Monuments to Eternity   3
   The ancient Newgrange and Carrowmore cemeteries. The
   Browneshill and Poulnabrone dolmens. Care of the soul at
   the dawn of civilization.

2. In the Footsteps of St. Patrick   17
   Armagh, Croagh Patrick, St. Patrick's Purgatory, the Rock
   of Cashel, and Ireland's conversion to Christianity.

3. Books, Bards, Monks, and Musicians   33
   The Book of Kells. Pub crawling in Dublin. Yeats and the
   faeries. Frank McCourt's Limerick. Blarney. Celtic music.
   Legendary and literary Ireland.

4. St. Kevin's Glorious Glendalough   51
   A storied Celtic monastery is green shrine to creation and
   the Creator.

5. Fortresses for Kin and Clan   63
   Dun Aengus. Dunbeg. Staigue Fort. Grianan of Aileach.
   Celtic family values in a harsh, heroic age.

6. Divine Outposts   75
   Remote Skellig Michael. Inishmurray. Monks search for
   silence and solitude on dozens of beautiful monastic islands.

 7. High Places and Thin Places   91
    Ancient hill forts, standing stones, and sacred wells reveal
    the Celts' love of the land and the pagan gods.

 8. Cities of God   105
    Monasteries and abbeys. Ciaran's Clonmacnois. Brigid's
    Kildare. Celtic crosses and round towers. Mellifont and
    Timoleague. Gallarus Oratory and Kylemore Abbey. Other
    saints' sacred sites.

 9. Pilgrims in Distant Lands   123
    St. Brendan the Navigator. Columba and Iona. Celtic saints
    in Europe. Pilgrimage to Knock. Wandering for God.

PART II: GETTING THERE

10. Tips for the Journey: General Information
    for Planning Your Trip   141
    Practical tips and helpful information about traveling in
    Ireland.

11. A–Z Guide: Sites, Cities, and Major Points
    of Interest   155
    A detailed alphabetical listing of hundreds of sites, cities,
    towns, hotels, B&Bs, and restaurants.

12. Suggested Itineraries   205
    Ideas for day trips and longer journeys.

    Recommended Resources   213
    Acknowledgments   218
    Index   219

Introduction

We knew very little about Ireland the first time we visited the island. Relying mainly on media coverage, we erroneously assumed that the entire island—both the independent southern Republic and the British-ruled north—was a tinderbox for the Troubles that have erupted between Catholics and Protestants in the north.

We read several tour books in an effort to learn more, but as we did so, we were a bit like hungry diners quickly trying to decipher a restaurant menu written in a mysterious language. Many of the places and events listed seemed to beckon to us, but we had little understanding of what they were or whether we would really enjoy them. Our itinerary for our first Ireland trip was a mishmash of breathtaking natural wonders, mystical ancient tombs, storied Celtic monastic sites, beautiful abbey ruins, and brazen tourist traps, all of which we tried to cram into a too-short schedule made even more harried by severe miscalculations about how many miles we could comfortably cover in a day on Ireland's narrow, winding roads.

Our efforts at preparation, though sincere, were woefully inadequate. Still, the island was gracious and welcoming. Its people were winsome and witty. Its wonders were so numerous and so intriguing that they astounded us, even in our ignorant state. Later—and we're not sure precisely when the realization dawned on us—we both knew that we had fallen deeply in love with this island, just as millions of others had done.

The book you now hold in your hands is our attempt to provide you with the information and background we wish we had had way back when.

Since that initial journey, we have returned to Ireland, both physically and intellectually, as often as possible. We have visited a growing number of unique and out-of-the-way sites, many of which have rewarded our efforts. Lois has accumulated a vast mountain of site information and travel tips. Steve devoured dozens of books on Irish spirituality, history, archaeology, myth, legend, literature, art, and music in order to write *In the House of Memory: Ancient Celtic Wisdom for Everyday Life*, an earlier book which explored the key spiritual principles of both Ireland's prehistoric pagan people and its Celtic Christian monks and saints. And in 1999, we began offering guided tours of the island.

Though still neophytes, we're far less ignorant than we once were. We hope the material we have gathered here is helpful and that you enjoy reading this book one-tenth as much as we enjoyed researching and writing it.

Celtic Revival

Recent years have witnessed an astounding growth of interest in all things Irish. The island, which has a population of some five million people, has long produced more than its share of brilliant literary giants, who as inheritors of the ancient Celtic gifts for eloquence and yarn-spinning, have created a vast international audience for novels, poems, and plays created by the Irish.

In the mid-nineteenth century, the devastating Irish famine led to the death of more than a million people and the emigration of a million more. In some parts of Ireland, one can still see the remains of the humble houses they left. Elsewhere, one of the lasting fruits of Irish immigration is the worldwide dissemination of Celtic music, a wonderful concoction of whimsy and sadness, sorrow and joy, which has attracted growing legions of loyal fans. In the mid-1990s, this interest in Celtic music and dance led to the surprise success of *Riverdance*, a dance revue, and its sequel, *Lord of the Dance*.

Though purists dismiss both shows as lowbrow "Celtic-Lite" entertainment, these performances sparked a renewed interest in Celtic culture that continues to be seen in increased CD sales of Celtic music, acclaimed Irish-themed films and plays like *Waking Ned Devine* and *Dancing at Lughnasa*, and growing enrollment in classes in traditional Irish dance, music, and language.

There's another area of Irish interest that had been bubbling under the surface for quite some time before becoming more pronounced in recent decades, and that's the intense curiosity many have about Celtic spirituality. Popular interest in religion and spirituality of all kinds has been growing in recent years, and spiritual themes have been appearing with greater frequency in movies, popular music, and books.

Ireland's spiritual legacy is wide and deep, encompassing both an ancient pagan stream and a more recent Christian element. For centuries, Ireland's splendid isolation allowed these two spiritual traditions to intermingle in many unique and fascinating ways. Just as *In the House of Memory* explored the underlying people and principles of Celtic spirituality, this book explores the places associated with those people and principles, helping the contemporary visitor understand more of the background of Ireland's numerous impressive sites.

It's impossible to predict whether the present-day interest in Ireland will continue to grow and deepen, or whether it will enjoy its brief moment in the spotlight before going the way of other short-lived trends. If we were betting people, we would predict a bright future and a continuing interest, encompassing both the trendy (a major women's fashion magazine recently featured an eighteen-page photo spread on Irish sweaters entitled "Celtic Chic") and the more substantial.

One thing's for sure, though: today's fascination with Celtic culture has helped fuel an unprecedented Irish travel boom. By the late nineties, nearly nine hundred thousand people were traveling from the United States to Ireland every year, more than double the numbers of a decade earlier. Among these pilgrims are millions of people of Irish descent who are visiting the island in an effort to reconnect with their ancestral roots.

The Irish travel boom means that visitors will be bumping up against more fellow foreigners than in former days, but there are also some benefits to the growth. For one thing, Irish authorities have spruced up many of their sites, building sparkling new visitors' centers near some, and adding interpretive centers or informative signs at others. In addition, there's an unprecedented number of options for lodging and dining, from quaint to extravagant.

There's been a change in the types of travel people are doing as well. As baby boomers come of age, there is a greater emphasis on travel that incorporates cultural, historical, and spiritual components. This book is designed to help travelers who have these interests make more out of their visit to Ireland.

Ireland 101

Before we really get going, you need to be aware of a few basic facts about Ireland and its history that will help you better understand and appreciate its sites. This is necessarily a superficial treatment of a complex subject, and if you would like to know more, we encourage you to consult some of the resources listed at the end of the book.

The Celts

Nearly everyone has heard of Celtic music, Celtic design, and Celtic culture, but few are familiar with the civilization that gave birth to all of these diverse and geographically distributed elements.

The Celts were an ancient Indo-European people who covered and conquered much of the known world in the centuries before the Romans ruled. Emerging from Asia and Russia in the millennium before the Christian era, they quickly overtook much of Europe, conquering Rome around 390 B.C.

They migrated to the British isles and Ireland by around 500 B.C. By the first century A.D., Rome had overtaken major Celtic strongholds in Europe and southern England, but the Romans never conquered Celtic outposts in Wales and Scotland, and they never even bothered invading Ireland, a land that was seen as remote and strategically unimportant. As a result, it is in these areas of the Celtic fringe—Ireland, Wales, Cornwall, and Scotland—that one can still find strong elements of Celtic culture.

Much of Western history has given the Celts a bad rap. Aristotle claimed that the Celtic soldiers, both men and women, fought naked, feared nothing, and were on occasion downright brutal. Romans portrayed Celts as primitive barbarians who fought by day and feasted all night. When St. Paul wrote his letter to the Christians in Galatia, he urged believers (in this pagan Celtic stronghold) to avoid idolatry, sorcery, hatred, and murder.

However, the Celts also possessed a flair for art and design, exhibited a love of language and literature, and were a deeply spiritual people. It wasn't until the fifth century that St. Patrick and other Christians came to Ireland and began writing down ancient Celtic myths and legends. All our knowledge of the Celts prior to Patrick comes from those who warred against them, and these were not entirely objective sources. Today, it's archaeologists studying the remains of Celtic culture who are filling in the significant blanks in the historical record.

Celtic Paganism

The Celtic people may have had a greater hunger for the divine than any other people the world has known. As Celtic scholar Anne Ross said at a 1978 conference on the Celtic consciousness,

A capacity for worship, religion, a passionate feeling for the supernatural, for the gods, or, later, God, is, I believe, the truest and most binding cultural element throughout the entire Celtic world.

In the centuries after Patrick, this spiritual impulse expressed itself through the Christian faith, a revealed religion based on the teachings of Jesus, the Old Testament prophets, and various New Testament writers. Celtic paganism, which still exists in many forms today, isn't a revealed religion but an older, more primitive form of spirituality which arose naturally among the Celts and other ancient rural people.

The term *pagan* comes from the Latin words *pagus*, a term urbane city dwellers used to describe an uncultivated rural area, and *paganus*, which they used to describe a person who lived in such a wild region. Similarly, *heathen* originally referred to a person who lived in the heaths, or open wastelands full of wild shrubs, including heather.

The paganism of the ancient Celtic people was a spontaneous expression of their sense that the world and everything in it, including themselves, was sacred. Or as twentieth-century neopagan Margot Adler expresses it, they subscribed to a simple, earth-based, nature faith she calls "radical pantheism." Adler described the basic tenets of paganism in her book *Drawing Down the Moon*.

The world is holy. Nature is holy. The body is holy. Sexuality is holy. The mind is holy. The imagination is holy. You are holy. . . . Divinity is immanent in all Nature. It is as much within you as without.

The Celts worshiped hundreds of pagan deities. Among the more widely known gods and goddesses was Danu, a mother goddess for whom the Danube River is named. The Celts believed that the earth on which they lived and depended was sacred, and that each force of nature, and possibly even each feature of the landscape, was wrapped up in divinity.

Celtic Christianity

Christianity had a minor presence in Ireland before Patrick came to preach there in 432 A.D., but Patrick and the Christians who came after him did something unique: they translated a complex and largely alien Christian theology into terms and concepts that were easily accessible to non-Christian Celts, often adapting pagan concepts and practices in the process.

Pagan Celts held a belief in the sacredness of the world. The Christians affirmed this belief, but added a unique Christian emphasis, explaining that the best way to understand the sacredness of creation was through a belief in an eternal Creator God, whose divinity is displayed in everything that is.

Instead of trying to convert the pagan Celts at the point of a sword, the Celtic Christians relied on reason and compassion. And if this strategy required them to reevaluate Christianity from top to bottom in order to assess how to make it meaningful to the pagans, doing so helped lead to a wonderful flowering of the faith. "Few forms of Christianity have offered an ideal of Christian perfection so pure as the Celtic Church of the sixth, seventh and eighth centuries," wrote Ernest Renan. The Catholic monk Thomas Merton agreed: "I am reading about Celtic monasticism, the hermits, the lyric poets, the pilgrims," he wrote. "A whole new world that has waited until now to open up for me."

A Guide to This Guide

We've designed this book to be helpful to you as you plan your own journey to Ireland. Here's how to get the most out of it.

The Major Sites

Following this introduction is Part I, which consists of nine chapters, each of which explores some of the more popular, interesting, or rewarding sites connected with a specific aspect of Celtic spirituality. Chapter 1, for example, examines pre-

historic tombs and cemeteries, which are some of the oldest
and most haunting pagan sites in Ireland. Chapter 2 evaluates
some of the many sites that have an association with St.
Patrick.

Ireland is a small island, but offers visitors a dazzling range
of hundreds of historic sites. We've tried to evaluate the
options and focus on those sites which are interesting and
rewarding to visit and which play an important role in at least
one aspect of Irish history and culture.

Take a few minutes to scan the Table of Contents, which
describes the kinds of sites covered in each chapter and the
historical period during which the sites were created or used.

Each of these nine chapters also includes a map showing
the location of the major sites. If you're trying to figure out
where you want to go in Ireland, you can scan the nine maps
to see which areas of the island have the greatest concentra-
tion of the kinds of sites you would like to see.

Getting There

Part II features a wealth of practical information designed
to help you find and enjoy the sites described in Part I. Chapter 10 includes general information about traveling in Ireland.
Chapter 11 is a detailed alphabetical guide to major sites and
nearby cities and towns. Included here is detailed information
about lodging, dining, and other practical matters. Chapter 12
features three sample itineraries to help you design your own
travel plans.

Finally, the resources section provides recommendations for
a number of books, videos, and other materials that can help
you learn more about Ireland, Celtic culture, and the sites
described in this book.

We wish we'd had some of this information at our fingertips
when we first began exploring Ireland, and we hope this book
makes your journey more enjoyable and more meaningful.

PART I
The Sites

Perpetual passage: Ancient people carved abstract spiral designs on this stone at the entrance to the Newgrange megalithic tomb. The window above the door admits sunlight into the heart of the tomb.

1

ꍏonuments to Eternity

Created thousands of years ago, Newgrange and Ireland's many other pre-Celtic tombs provide a powerful link with the distant past. These massive monuments also illustrate the dawning of one of humanity's foundational spiritual beliefs: the immortality of the soul.

Unearthing Ancient Traditions

The first humans appeared in Ireland some ten thousand years ago. A few thousand years later, their descendants were honoring their dead by building massive stone tombs, many of them prominently placed on hilltops or other sacred places.

Today, anyone willing to travel thirty-two miles north of the high-tech hustle and bustle of Dublin's international airport can enter Newgrange, the most impressive of Ireland's hundreds of huge tombs, and one of the world's oldest and most amazing monuments.

Newgrange (which is also known by its ancient Celtic name, Bru na Boinne) is said to be the burial place of many of

Ireland's High Kings, who ruled regions of the island in the centuries before the arrival of St. Patrick in the fifth century. The monument also figures prominently in ancient Celtic mythology. Largely forgotten during the Middle Ages, the monument was rediscovered by a local landowner in 1699, and has amazed visitors and scientists ever since. One writer praised Newgrange as "perhaps the most celebrated and enigmatic sacred monument on earth." Certainly, few sites anywhere in the world offer visitors easier access to such a palpable experience of an ancient civilization.

Centuries older than Egypt's pyramids, Newgrange was constructed nearly 5,000 years ago out of tons of hand-hefted earth and hundreds of huge stones in a project so massive that completing it must have required millions of man-hours. Unlike Egyptian pyramids, each of which was built to house a single pharaoh, Newgrange and Ireland's other major tombs were lovingly created to house the remains of small groups of the dead. Excavations conducted on these tombs in recent decades have revealed a combination of cremated human remains and bones laid to rest amid small collections of both mundane and mystical items, which were believed to assist the soul in its transition to another world. Carbon-dating tests even suggest that some of the Irish tombs may be humanity's earliest shrines to the belief in the afterlife and the existence of the soul.

Newgrange is far older than England's more popular Stonehenge, a monument with which it has many intriguing similarities. As far as we know, Stonehenge was designed for rituals, not burials. Though they were intended for different purposes, the two monuments represent impressive achievements of megalithic (or "great stone") construction. Ancient Stone Age people erected thousands of megalithic tombs, stone circles, and other memorials throughout Ireland, England, Scotland, and the westernmost fringes of Europe. Ireland has more than a thousand megalithic sites, many of which are well preserved and easily accessible. This chapter explores some

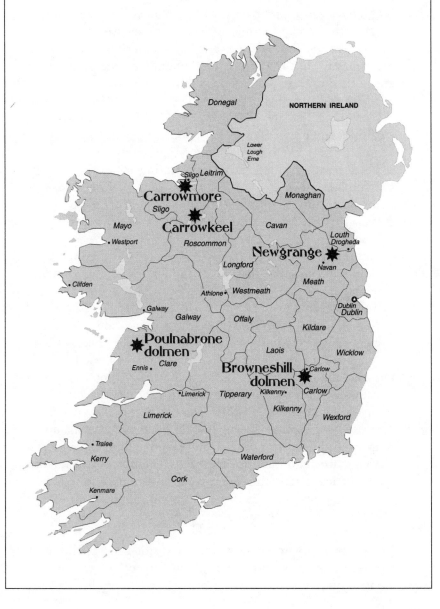

ANCIENT TOMBS

of Ireland's major megalithic tombs and cemeteries, while chapter 7 will examine its stone circles.

There's yet another powerful resonance between Stonehenge, whose majestic megaliths tower over England's Salisbury plain, and Newgrange, a circular structure that is much more massive but is mostly buried under tons and tons of rock and dirt. Both monuments come alive in an unusual way on the Winter Solstice (December 21 or 22 every year, depending on the calendar), a day that was held in reverence and awe by Europe's ancient pagan people. On this, the shortest day of the year, the sun's dawning rays illuminate central areas of these two monuments, demonstrating in powerful ways that prehistoric engineers used the most precise measurements and cautious building techniques in order to honor the spiritual connection believed to exist between earth and heaven.

Although Newgrange has superficial similarities to many ancient structures, this massive monument represents a unique contribution to our understanding of human spirituality and sacred geography.

Unfortunately, we know next to nothing about who the ancient megalithic builders were, what they believed, or how the monuments they created fit into their daily lives. It's obvious, though, that they lavished much greater time and attention upon their massive memorials and shrines than they did their own residences, of which there are virtually no significant surviving remains. It was as if these people placed a much higher premium on creating solid and long-lasting sacred spaces that would benefit the dead in eternity than they did on constructing the humble quarters which housed the living.

A Timeless Tomb

In its heyday, Newgrange would have stood out as the most spectacular monument in the sacred Boyne Valley. The site of many important chapters in Ireland's history, the smooth-flowing River Boyne was believed by ancient pagan people to be the home of the goddess Boann.

Today, aerial views of the Newgrange tomb make it look like a huge, unevenly shaped circle of cheese, or even a squat, lopsided cake. Situated on the highest point on a long, low ridge, the tomb rises to an average height of 36 feet and has an average diameter of 300 feet. Its front is decorated with hundreds of bright, polished quartz stones which make the monument visible for miles around. These were quarried in the Wicklow hills some forty miles away. The base of the entire mound is encircled by ninety-seven large kerbstones. These heavy Stonehenge-sized rocks, which were quarried some ten miles away, aren't standing upright; rather they are lying on their sides, giving the mound an attractive, well-defined border.

Surrounding the mound, like a silent sentry, stood a stone circle that archaeologists believe may have consisted of as many as thirty-five huge upright boulders, enclosing an area of about two acres. Today, only a handful of these boulders survive. Some were probably used over the centuries in paving or building projects, while others may have been destroyed by religious zealots, who in centuries past made an avocation of obliterating prehistoric pagan sites.

The most amazing aspects of Newgrange can't be seen from the outside, though. Probing its deeper mysteries requires a journey through a narrow sixty-foot passageway that takes one to the inner recesses of the tomb. In years past, visitors could drive their cars to a small parking area near the mound and enter at will. Today, regular guided tours start at the impressive new Bru na Boinne visitors center, which opened in 1997. These tours escort growing numbers of tourists under the tons of earth and rock into the central burial chamber that was the holy of holies of this massive monument.

It's not a journey for the claustrophobic. If you're of average build, your shoulders brush against some of the forty-plus upright stone megaliths as you travel through the passageway.

And if you're of average height, you'll have to bend down in order to fit under some of the huge stone slabs which rest on the megaliths and make up the roof of the passageway.

The passageway opens into a cross-shaped chamber area featuring a central room that can comfortably hold up to two dozen visitors. Radiating off from this central area are three smaller recessed chambers. It was in one of these recesses that archaeologists, studying the tomb during the 1960s, found a large stone basin containing cremated human remains. Today, as one stands in the cool, dark central chamber, gazing up at the massive stone roof twenty feet above, it's difficult not to marvel at the skill of the ancient engineers and architects who created this stony sanctuary.

While most of the outer portions of the monument have been painstakingly rebuilt over the last few decades, portions of the passageway and all of the central chamber remain unaltered from the time they were created some 5,000 years ago. This handmade mound was the product of years of back-breaking labor conducted by a large, settled, and highly organized population. At a time when the average human life span was around thirty years, the creation of such a massive memorial would have required a vast social investment and intense cooperation.

Pausing for a moment within the funereal central chamber, one can almost sense the magnitude of the ages, not to mention the massive weight of the monument itself. Created millennia before Europe's great cathedral builders used architectural innovations like the arch and the gable to erect tall and majestic sanctuaries, Newgrange features a much older technique known as corbelling. The central chamber's corbelled roof features large rock slabs laid atop one another. In each successive layer, the slabs are extended a bit further over the opening, until they meet at the top and enclose the whole chamber. The stone roof was then covered and sealed with dirt and rocks, but not before ancient irrigation specialists carved a series of expertly designed drainage grooves in the rocks. Thanks to this ingenious system, the chamber has remained amazingly dry through fifty centuries.

But Newgrange is far more than a prehistoric engineering marvel; it is also an ancient artistic masterpiece. Many of the rocks that make up the monument's kerbstones, passageway megaliths, and chamber stones are decorated with elaborate and amazingly contemporary-looking abstract carvings. The designs are varied, but one of the most common motifs is the spiral, which some archaeologists speculate may have been a symbol representing eternal life. Inside the central chamber is a beautiful carving featuring three interlocking spirals. Additional stones are decorated with zigzag lines, lozenges, and other geometric forms. While most of the designs are incised into the stones, a few are carved in relief.

During the Winter Solstice, as the sun rises it sends shafts of bright light streaming into the tomb through a small opening above the door, illuminating both the passageway and the inner burial chamber with a brilliant warm glow. This stunning light show, whose effects are simulated during guided tours of the monument, lasts only seventeen minutes of one day every year, although the sun also illuminates the chamber for shorter periods in the days immediately before and after the Winter Solstice.

For the people who lived in the vicinity of Newgrange, the annual penetration of the sun's rays into the tomb's central chamber must have communicated much more than the anticipated return of spring and summer, as important as this was for an agrarian population. Beyond this potent symbol of the earth's seasonal cycles, Newgrange also spoke to them of the cycles of human life: of death and rebirth. This monument reflects the timeless human hope that even after death, life will continue on in some form.

In addition, the area surrounding Newgrange is so rich in sites from so many important periods of Irish and Celtic history that it might be worthwhile making Dublin a base for excursions into the countryside. Among the nearby sites, many of which we will be examining in more detail later, are the Hills of Tara and Slane, the town of Kells, Monasterboice, and Mellifont Abbey.

From Tomb to Necropolis

Newgrange is more than an isolated tomb. Rather, it is the hub of a much larger complex of megalithic structures which together form what archaeologists call a necropolis, or city of the dead. In a pattern used by many Stone Age builders, tombs were grouped together in sacred precincts. Less than a mile away from Newgrange lies the tomb known as Dowth, which contains two separate passage tombs under its big mound. Less than a mile up the river is Knowth, surrounded by seventeen additional smaller satellite tombs, which hover around the larger Knowth tomb like planets around the sun. Dowth is not open to visitors, but can be seen from the road. The Knowth tomb and complex is open to visitors through the Bru na Boinne visitors center.

Together, Newgrange, Dowth, Knowth, and their related satellite tombs give the visitor an idea of how important burial rituals must have been to the ancient people who built these shrines. But the Newgrange necropolis isn't the most impressive in Ireland. That honor belongs to the Carrowmore megalithic cemetery, which some archaeologists believe was the largest necropolis of the ancient world.

Also known by its ancient Celtic name Ceathru Mor, which means "great quarter," and located on the northwestern coast of Ireland just south of the city of Sligo, the Carrowmore site is believed by some researchers to have housed as many as two hundred separate tombs in its time. Over the millennia, many of these tombs have been destroyed by farming or quarrying, but around forty of the Carrowmore monuments have been preserved and can be visited. Guided tours and interpretive displays are offered at the visitors center, which opened in 1990.

Seen individually, none of the Carrowmore tombs are quite as impressive as Newgrange. The Carrowmore necropolis is centuries older than Newgrange, and the techniques used to construct the tombs here were more primitive. In fact, tests conducted by a Swedish archaeological team indicate that the earliest of the Carrowmore tombs may have been built some

Visitors learn about the history of the Carrowmore megalithic complex, which is Ireland's largest—and possibly oldest—ancient necropolis.

seven thousand years ago. If true, this could make these tombs the oldest man-made structures on earth.*

What makes the Carrowmore complex so interesting is its age combined with the fact that from nearly any spot in the entire necropolis, one is surrounded by ancient tombs. Even the mountains in the distance are topped with megalithic monuments, which were designed to be seen from the Carrowmore cemetery. The largest of these monuments is the massive tomb traditionally ascribed to Celtic warrior-queen Medhbh, which sits atop nearby Knocknarea, where it towers over both Carrowmore and Sligo Bay.

Some of the Carrowmore tombs are earlier versions of the Newgrange-type passage style monuments, which feature a passageway leading to a central chamber. Ireland has nearly two hundred passage tombs. However, most of the Carrowmore tombs are the so-called dolmen (or portal) style. There are nearly a thousand dolmen tombs in Ireland. These con-

*The findings of the Swedish archaeological team can be accessed at their Web site, www.hgo.se/carrowmore.

sist of three or more large standing stones topped off by a larger stone, which is perched upon the standing stones and serves as a roof.

One of the best preserved of the Carrowmore dolmen tombs is tomb seven, which consists of six large boulders. The tomb is surrounded by a stone circle made up of thirty-one boulders. Excavations conducted during the 1970s found large amounts of human remains, as well as decorative pins carved out of antlers that resembled mushrooms. Also interesting is tomb fifty-one, which was one of Carrowmore's largest tombs, and may have been a centerpiece of the necropolis. The large roof slab which covers the chamber area of tomb fifty-one features curved carvings which look like predecessors of Newgrange's more fully developed spirals and designs.

When they were originally built, the large rocks of the dolmen tombs were covered by additional smaller rocks and dirt, enclosing the burial chambers inside. Over the centuries these materials have disappeared, leaving the tombs' massive stone skeletons, which sometimes resemble tables. The word *dolmen* is really a misnomer. The term is a Breton word which means "stone table," which reflects earlier misguided beliefs that the dolmens were some kind of druid altars, not Stone Age tombs. As archaeologists have learned more about these structures, it has become increasingly clear what the tombs would have looked like when they were originally created.

Some of Ireland's dolmen tombs are so delicate looking that it seems the roof stones might fall off their rocky pedestals with the slightest nudge. But appearances can be deceiving, and Ireland's dolmen tombs have proven surprisingly sturdy. One dolmen tomb, located just across the street from the Carrowmore visitors center, was struck by an automobile whose driver failed to properly navigate a curve. The tomb barely budged. The driver was killed. Some of the huge tombs are surprisingly close to the narrow, curving roads.

A few miles south of Sligo is the Carrowkeel megalithic complex. Though smaller than Carrowmore, it contains many impressive tombs.

County Sligo also contains the ruins of two of the most impressive examples of a third type of Stone Age burial site: the court tomb. One writer has described court tombs as resembling a lobster's claw—an apt description of the Creevykeel court tomb, located a few miles north of Sligo and one of the finest examples of the type. Court tombs featured numerous burial compartments and an adjacent round-shaped court, which may have been a site where memorial rituals were performed.

Two fine examples of a fourth kind of ancient tomb, the wedge tomb, are also found in County Sligo. There is also another well preserved passage tomb at Knocknarea. The archaeologically rich County Sligo also has many excellent examples of the kinds of sites we will be discussing in later chapters, including hill fort complexes, an impressive promontory fort, holy wells, and unique grave slabs from early in the Christian era. When weather permits, boat rides can be arranged to Inishmurray, one of Ireland's best-preserved island monastery complexes (see chapter 6). Information on these sites is available in the booklet "Archeology in County Sligo," found at the Carrowmore visitors center, or at the North West Tourism office in Sligo town.

Touring the Tombs

While numerous tombs are clustered in the Newgrange and Carrowmore complexes, there are a handful of Irish tombs that stand alone and are worth a brief visit.

Undoubtedly, the most unusual is the Browneshill dolmen tomb, which stands in a cow pasture near the town of Carlow in County Carlow. There's nothing unusual about its design: upright stones holding a larger roof stone. What is unusual is the sheer size and estimated weight (one hundred tons) of the roof stone. This is reportedly the heaviest capstone in Europe. Trying to figure out how ancient engineers moved it to this spot and placed it atop the other stones boggles the mind.

The Poulnabrone dolmen, situated amid the otherworldly looking limestone of the Burren region in County Clare, has a much different allure. Made of limestone uprights capped by a wing-shaped limestone roof, the tomb looks more as if it could take off in flight. Located less than twenty miles from the scenic Cliffs of Moher, one of Ireland's most visited natural attractions, the Poulnabrone is within easy reach of thousands of tourists.

Other unique tombs include the Proleek dolmen in County Louth, and the Lough Gur necropolis in County Limerick, which is part of a larger complex of ancient pagan sites.

Mysterious Monuments

Whether they are huge or humble and gathered in groups or situated in lonely isolation, Ireland's ancient tombs can have a powerful impact on the visitor who is willing to seek them out and consider their mysteries.

Why did Stone Age people devote so much of their time and resources to building massive, magnificent resting places for their dead? It is intriguing to contrast the size and durability of their earlier monuments with the much smaller and simpler shrines we build today to honor our own dead. Could it be that our ancient ancestors placed a much greater emphasis on what comes after this earthly life ends? How different from ours must their view of the world have been, since their social geography was dominated by monumental reminders of death, a subject most moderns would rather ignore?

It is also worthwhile to consider the important philosophical and theological implications of burying the dead. Eons before humanity had any clear notion of religion and millennia before the world's major theistic faiths were born, primitive people came to the conclusion that some essential part of us all survives death. The eternal structures they built celebrated the fundamental belief that whatever this essence was, its continuance was something sacred. And this belief called forth a flurry of monument building that provides us with the only evidence that these people ever existed.

Scholars who specialize in archaeology and ancient history are currently involved in intense debates over when beliefs about the immortality of the soul first appeared, and how the technology used by tomb builders migrated around the globe.

Megalithic tombs appear throughout western Europe, with the notable exception of England and Scotland, where they are relatively rare. There are thousands of ancient tombs in France, and thousands more in Denmark and Sweden. Many also appear in the western and southern regions of Spain. There are intriguing similarities in the way tombs were engineered and constructed as well as the creative ways in which they were decorated.

Did a belief in the afterlife spontaneously appear in all of these regions? And did tomb-making skills develop independently in each place in total isolation from people employing similar techniques in other areas of the world? Some scholars don't think so, and argue instead that there was a diffusion of beliefs and techniques from one area to the others. Whether this is so and where it all began are questions that may be unanswerable by science. The tomb builders who lived so long ago left their amazing handiwork, and this may be all we ever know of them.

Still, in some parts of Ireland, some of the people who are studying the island's ancient monuments will—in an unguarded moment—tell you that they're convinced that the world's ancient burial practices began in their country and spread out from there. Some say radio carbon tests have already proved as much, while others say the data are inconclusive. As we'll see later in this book when we examine some of Ireland's better known monastic graveyards, many of which feature numerous large, intricately carved Celtic crosses, the Irish long continued to devote significant time and energy to honoring the dead.

Regardless of when—or if—the scientific evidence ever materializes, Ireland's ancient Stone Age shrines still speak of immortality and faith to those who are willing to search them out.

Statues of Patrick, like this one atop the Hill of Slane, show the saint's continuing influence on Ireland's people and culture.

2

In the Footsteps of St. Patrick

Fifteen centuries ago, a man named Patrick came to Ireland, igniting the island's wholesale conversion from paganism to Christianity. Today, reminders of the work of Ireland's patron saint can be seen throughout the land.

A Peaceful Revolution

The two major influences on Celtic spirituality are paganism and Christianity. As we have seen, Ireland's pre-Celtic Stone Age builders, some of them working seven thousand years ago, left a lasting legacy of megalithic monuments all across the land. In more recent times, the only group to rival these early pagans in their zeal for things both spiritual and architectural are the disciples of St. Patrick, a man who came to Ireland in 432 A.D. because he believed God called him to do so. In the process he ushered in a widespread conversion to the Christian faith that may be the most peaceful religious transformation of a country in human history.

From majestic cathedrals in Dublin and Armagh, to rugged and demanding pilgrimage sites in the country's northern and western regions, reminders of Patrick's life and ministry can be seen all over Ireland. In this chapter we will be examining some of the most important of these sites, but first, let's review the life of Patrick and consider the lasting impact he has had upon this country.

From Slavery to Service

We don't know much about the beliefs of Patrick's pagan predecessors. They shied away from writing things down, relying on oral tradition to pass on their ancient traditions and instruct their followers. With the arrival of Patrick on the scene, however, Ireland's recorded history begins. Patrick was the first of Ireland's many highly literate Christian saints, writing two documents that have survived through the ages: his *Confession*, and his *Letter to the Soldiers of Coroticus*. There's still plenty of myth and fantasy wrapped up in some of the legends concerning Patrick, particularly the stories about his alleged use of the three-leaf clover for a teaching aid, or his banishing all of the snakes from the country. Still, with the arrival of Patrick on the scene, we can finally, for the first time, begin separating legend and myth from historical fact.

Unfortunately, we don't know very much about Patrick's early life. He was born in Roman-ruled England some time between 370 and 390 A.D. to a man named Calpurnius—a Roman tax official, a relatively well-off landowner, and a dedicated church member. Patrick exhibited the typical adolescent disdain for the faith of his father. "I did not know the true God," he writes in his *Confession*.

That all changed when a gang of Irish marauders raided England, captured Patrick, and hauled him off to Ireland, where he spent the next six years as a slave and herdsman. Separated from his loved ones and forced to live among people whose language and customs seemed curious at best, Patrick turned to God. "In a single day I would say as many as a hundred prayers, and almost as many at night," he writes. When he was about twenty-two years old, Patrick received a dramatic supernatural vision in which God told him to flee his servitude. "See, your ship is ready," a voice told him, leading to a harrowing two-hundred-mile overland journey and a risk-filled ocean voyage.

Then, once again, the biographical record goes blank. Tradition says Patrick studied theology, perhaps on the European mainland, before being ordained and returning to England. The storyline picks up again when, instead of settling down into a peaceful life among family and friends, Patrick receives another vision, this one leading him to return to Ireland to serve the very people who had once imprisoned him:

> I saw in the night the vision of a man whose name was Victoricus, coming as it were from Ireland, with countless letters. And he gave me one of them, and I read the opening words of the letter, which were the voice of the Irish, and as I read the beginning of the letter I thought that at the same moment I heard their voice . . . and thus did they cry out as with one mouth: We ask thee, boy, come and walk among us once more.

Patrick wasn't the first Christian to be dispatched to Ireland, but the impression one gets of his predecessors is that they were an early version of the hackneyed portrait of the well-meaning but self-defeating missionary who sailed off to foreign shores and forced the natives to abandon their traditions.

Patrick was different. He had studied the Irish at close range for six years. He understood something of their pagan ways and ancient myths, seeing in them signs of a deep and often unsatisfied spiritual hunger. He devoted the rest of his life to traveling and teaching in their midst, writing:

> Should I be worthy, I am prepared to give even my life without hesitation and most gladly for His name, and it is in

Ireland that I wish to spend it until I die, if the Lord would grant it to me.

Perhaps it should come as no surprise, then, that Patrick's mission to Ireland, which began in 432 A.D. and ended with his death in 461 A.D., would prove to be one of the most successful ministries in human history.

The Irish people were traumatized by the warfare and bloodshed of their so-called "heroic" era; they were fed up with the mercurial nature of their pagan gods; and they were intrigued by the way Patrick customized the universals of the Gospel message to their particular culture. They embraced the Christian message wholeheartedly. The conversion of Ireland was both a top-down change instituted by various Celtic kings as well as a bottom-up change initiated by thousands of common folk. Altogether, this transformation led to an amazing flowering of Celtic Christianity which one writer described as "a Christianity so pure and serene as . . . could hardly be equaled and never repeated."

Thanks to Patrick's own writings, as well as centuries-old traditions that have grown up around his life and work, it's possible for the modern traveler to retrace some of the saint's amazing pilgrimage on the island.

Our knowledge remains partial, though. For example, we don't know where in England Patrick was born, and there are conflicting claims about where he is buried. Also, it's not certain where Patrick served out his six years of involuntary servitude in Ireland, although many of the oldest traditions point to the rugged Slemish Mountains in County Antrim, the northeasternmost area of Northern Ireland.

There's much more certainty concerning the major sites described below, which were connected with the thirty years Patrick spent ministering in Ireland. Stopping at some of these places can give the visitor a deeper appreciation of the transformation that occurred in Ireland some fifteen centuries ago.

PATRICK'S PATH

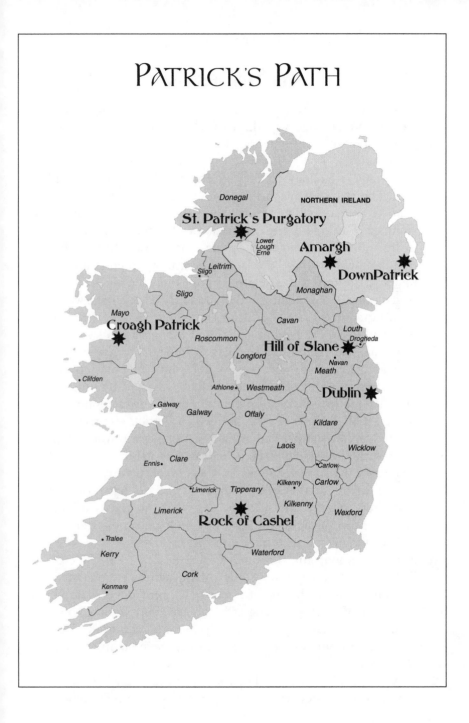

The Hill of Slane

This grassy, windswept hill located just a stone's throw northwest of Newgrange was the site of one of the earliest and most important confrontations between Patrick and Ireland's pagan priests.

Beltane, a holiday celebrated on May 1, was the second most important event on the pagan Celts' religious calendar. Beltane was a fertility festival that celebrated the return of summer. The traditional celebration called for all the people in Ireland to snuff out their candles and household fires, letting darkness overtake the land. Then, in an important ceremony at the top of the nearby Hill of Tara (see chapter 7), a pagan priest would light the Beltane fire, and this light would then be spread throughout the land. The Beltane fire was believed to rid the land of ghosts and the diseases of winter.

In 433, one year after he arrived in Ireland, Patrick issued a direct challenge to the pagans and their celebrations by ascending the Hill of Slane on Beltane eve and igniting his own flaming fire, this one celebrating the Christian holiday of Easter. This defiant act, through which Patrick was trying to show that Christianity had arrived in Ireland and would contend with the island's pagan beliefs, has made the Hill of Slane a sacred site ever since. St. Erc, one of the lesser known of the many early Celtic saints, is said to have built a monastery on the spot. Today, there are no traces of this monastery, or of the medieval abbey built centuries later.

Instead, anyone who travels to this little-visited site today can walk among the remains of a Franciscan friary. There's little left of the friary now, but a dark, narrow circular stairway takes one to the top of a tower that provides a dramatic panorama of the hill, its cemetery, and the surrounding countryside. The rustic ruins of an adjacent college, founded in 1540, feature numerous rooms, many of them complete with fireplaces.

A statue of Patrick has been built on the site where tradition says his Easter fire was lit. Standing on the hill, one can imagine how Patrick's fire would have shone like a beacon on that dark night centuries ago.

Armagh

Towering over the skyline of this storied city are two competing cathedrals of St. Patrick—one Anglican and one Catholic—that face each other from opposing hillsides less than a half mile apart. The existence of these two impressive ecclesiastical edifices speaks volumes about both the universal appeal of Patrick and the divisiveness of Irish cultural and religious life over the past few centuries.

The Anglican church has the closest historic connections to the saint, who made Armagh the administrative base of his operations and built his first stone church here in the fifth century. Patrick may have chosen this location because of the town's long association with Ireland's pre-Christian pagan culture. (The name Armagh comes from the Irish Ard Mhacha, which means Macha's Height, referring to the legendary pagan queen who ruled here. Some have even suggested that Armagh may be Ireland's oldest city.)

None of Patrick's original building remains, but much of a later medieval version does. The church's west wall features a tablet marking the burial place of Irish High King Brian Boru, who vanquished the Vikings in 1014. Over the centuries, the church structure has continued to evolve, and during the English Reformation it became affiliated with the Church of Ireland.

During much of the seventeenth, eighteenth, and nineteenth centuries, Ireland's Catholics were oppressed and hounded. Practicing Catholic rites was illegal, and priests were jailed or worse. The terror ended with Catholic Emancipation in 1828. Within a few years, Armagh was once again home to a Catholic Archbishop—the first in three hundred years—who began a building program. The foundation stone for the Catholic cathedral was laid in 1840, but soon Ireland was in the grip of its horrible potato famine, which led to the death or emigration of up to two million people. Work on the cathedral resumed in 1854 and the building was finally dedicated in 1873.

Today, the Catholic Cathedral of St. Patrick is a wonder to behold. From the intricate and beautiful flooring made of thousands of mosaic tiles, to the lofty, sky-blue ceiling, the church is a magnificent work of design and devotion that rivals medieval cathedrals. High above the nave are medallions featuring the patron saints of twenty Irish dioceses, whose beatific faces beam down at the visitor from their gold backgrounds. Additional artistic touches are found in the cathedral's marble altars; its finely carved stations of the cross; and its majestic stained-glass windows, which give a visual summary of some of the highlights of Ireland's religious history.

Spending a few moments in the shimmering glory of this cathedral makes one forget, at least temporarily, about the Troubles which have bedeviled Armagh and much of Northern Ireland for decades, and which have turned the town of Portadown, a few short miles up the road, into a battlefield for long-simmering disputes between Protestant loyalists and Catholic nationalists.

While in Armagh, if you want to know more about Patrick or the history of the city, you can pay a visit to the Saint Patrick's Trian Visitor Complex, which features a hodgepodge of displays and facilities.

Croagh Patrick

Far away from the citified confines of Armagh is the rough and rugged beauty of Ireland's western coast. Located near the bustling town of Westport and overlooking scenic Clew Bay stands towering Croagh Patrick, a bald and rocky mountain that is the scene of an annual pilgrimage dedicated to the island country's patron saint.

Legend has it that Patrick climbed the conical 2,500-foot-tall mountain, staying atop the rugged peak for forty days and

Rough and rocky Croagh Patrick has been a popular pilgrimage site for more than a thousand years.

forty nights, praying and fasting and asking God for special spiritual blessings for the Irish people. Today, scholars debate the legend's validity. Did Patrick really scale the mountain, or does the account merely represent well-meaning believers' efforts to enthrone Patrick alongside biblical figures like Moses (who met God on a mountain), and Jesus (who fasted and prayed for forty days in the desert)?

The debate continues, but once a year, thousands of people bring life to the legend by climbing to the top of Croagh Patrick in honor of the saint. They call it Reek Sunday, and it's held the last Sunday of July. In some years, as many as thirty thousand people make the climb. The young and the old, the physically fit and the frail, all attempt to scale the mountain, reciting prayers and Hail Marys along the way, and pausing at the top for Mass before beginning their descent.

The spiritually adventurous add to the pilgrimage's punch by walking barefoot up the mountain, which, with its loose, rough rock is difficult enough to climb with thick-soled hiking boots. In the nineteenth century, the climb was even tougher. Then, tradition required the hardiest souls to climb the last one hundred feet of the ascent on their hands and knees, praying a final round of three hundred prayers as they made their slow, painful progress.

The Christian legends about Croagh Patrick developed soon after St. Patrick's death. Within a few centuries, pilgrims erected a simple sanctuary atop the peak, which has since been replaced by a newer structure. There's also ample evidence that Ireland's pagan people probably honored the mountain as a sacred site long before the Christian era; and interestingly, some scholars have pointed out that the last Sunday in July was close to the date when the pagan festival of Lughnasa, honoring the god Lugh, was typically held.

Borrowing from earlier pagan traditions makes some Christians uneasy, but it didn't worry St. Patrick, who made a regular practice of appropriating some of paganism's foundational myths, heroes, and holy places and reinterpreting them in Christian terms, thereby explaining the new faith to the followers of the old religions.

Allegedly, Patrick even appropriated the pagan practice of circle rituals, in which pagan priests and priestesses invoked spiritual powers from the four corners of the earth. Patrick and later Celtic Christian saints were famous for their circling prayers, which believers recited as they faced north, then east, then south, then west. The best known of all the Celtic prayers is "St. Patrick's Breastplate," so called because it and similar prayers were thought to protect the believer with God's divine power. For centuries, pilgrims making the trek up Croagh Patrick have recited the Breastplate as they climb. The mountain's pinnacle, with its panoramic view of this beautiful corner of Ireland, seems like a perfect spot to recite one of the prayer's final stanzas:

> Christ with me, Christ before me, Christ behind me,
> Christ in me, Christ beneath me, Christ above me,
> Christ on my right, Christ on my left,
> Christ where I lie, Christ where I sit, Christ where
>   I arise,
> Christ in the heart of every man who thinks of me,
> Christ in the mouth of every man who speaks of me,
> Christ in every eye that sees me,
> Christ in every ear that hears me.

St. Patrick's Purgatory

Climbing Croagh Patrick is a walk in the park compared to the privations endured by the thousands of pilgrims who subject themselves to a pilgrimage at St. Patrick's Purgatory, located on tiny Station Island in Lough Derg, east of the town of Donegal. There's no proof Patrick ever visited the island, though he is supposed to have founded a monastery on the nearby shore. Still, within a century of his death it had already become an important spot for spiritual retreats. And in the succeeding centuries, layers of accumulated legend turned the site into one of Europe's foremost Christian destinations. On maps dating from the time of Christopher Columbus, the Purgatory is portrayed as the most important site in Ireland.

According to the twelfth-century Latin manuscript *Tractatus de Purgatorio sancti Patricii*, which was written by a monk at the English monastery of Sartis, it all began when Jesus appeared to Patrick during the saint's forty-day sojourn on Croagh Patrick, took him to a deserted place, and showed him a dark, round pit, or cave, saying, "Whoever, being truly repentant and armed with true faith, would enter this pit and remain for the duration of one day and one night, would be purged of all the sins of his life." People believed the pit was a doorway to other worlds, revealing the glories of heaven and the terrors of hell. Or, as the author of the *Tractatus* put it, "Here those who have lived in this life with some sins, but are nevertheless just and destined for eternal life, will be tormented for a time in order to be purified."

Promising results like these, it's no wonder the Purgatory has for centuries been an immensely popular spot for pilgrims. What's even more amazing is that as many as thirty thousand people still go to the island between May and September every year to participate in either a one-day retreat or a three-day pilgrimage. Those hardy enough to attempt the pilgrimage endure a harsh regimen of fasting, all-night prayer sessions, numerous worship services, and lengthy stretches of barefoot walking around the many circular "beds" (or pits) where saints of earlier days were believed to have spent hours in prayer.

Maureen Boyle helps process the thousands of requests from people wanting to participate in the Lough Derg events. "There are as many reasons for 'doing' Lough Derg as there are pilgrims," she says. "Each person comes to the Island with his own particular reason." Boyle says many come to thank God for blessings received, while others come to request a special blessing for themselves or loved ones. Still others go to Lough Derg once a year for an annual period of renewal and reevaluation. "The vast majority of those who come here go away feeling renewed, refreshed," says Boyle, and they leave "with hope and courage to face the future."

Visitors to Station Island must register to take part in one of the one-day retreats or three-day pilgrimages. Doing so connects the modern-day pilgrim to a tradition that has continued, in a variety of forms, for nearly fifteen centuries. Even though the Purgatory is steeped in tradition, interested people can investigate it through a Web site (www.iol.ie/~lochderg). Unfortunately, the original purgatorial cave is no longer accessible.

Cashel (St. Patrick's Rock)

Peter Harbison, who has probably written more about Ireland's archaeology and historic sites than any other living person, calls the Rock of Cashel "the most dramatic of all Irish monuments."

Sometime during the fourth century, a group of Irish knights built fortifications upon the rock, which rises gracefully from the plains of southern Ireland northeast of Waterford. St. Patrick visited the area in the fifth century, and made it into a bishopric.

One of the most celebrated legends connected with the site involves Patrick's relationship with King Aenghus, who ruled the Munster region during the saint's lifetime. Patrick routinely met with Irish kings as he traveled around the country. In part, such contacts were goodwill gestures designed to ensure his ability to continue traveling and teaching, but Patrick also talked to the kings about Christianity and sought their conversion to the faith. Aenghus, for one, accepted Patrick's invitation, and later agreed to be baptized. According to the legend, Patrick accidentally pierced the king's foot with his staff. The king bore the injury with a royal stiff upper lip, mistakenly assuming that the stabbing was a part of the baptismal ritual.

For the next thousand years, the rock served as center stage in some of the most important episodes in Irish history. High

King Brian Boru was crowned here in 977, and made Cashel
his capital. Granted to the church in 1101, the rock now features the remains of a cathedral which was built during the
thirteenth century and was badly damaged by the intense
rivalries that enveloped the area in later centuries. Today, a
museum and visitors center are on the grounds, which feature
the remains of the cathedral as well as two abbeys.

Other Sites

St. Patrick's Cathedral, Dublin

One of two striking medieval Protestant cathedrals located
less than a mile apart in the center of Ireland's capital city, St.
Patrick's has the closest ties to the saint, who allegedly baptized converts in a well there. In 1901, excavations uncovered
a stone slab which had long covered the well. Visitors can visit
the site of the well in an attractive park next to the church,
while the stone slab is one of dozens of interesting items on
display within the church.

Founded as a Catholic church, St. Patrick's was taken over
by the Church of Ireland following the English Reformation.
A number of displays are devoted to the cathedral's most
famous dean, Jonathan Swift, author of *Gulliver's Travels* and
other works, who is buried here a few feet away from his
beloved wife, Stella. A small admission fee allows visitors to
stroll through the beautiful church, which has many architectural similarities to England's Salisbury Cathedral. Visitors can
also attend one of St. Patrick's Sunday services or some of the
many other functions the church hosts, including weeknight
evensong services and a regular schedule of organ recitals.

Downpatrick

This Northern Ireland town boasts that it has St. Patrick's
grave, but is the boast true? We may never know. Still, Down

Cathedral is attractive, and the town's museum includes a St. Patrick Heritage Center which gives a visual depiction of the high points of the saint's life and features a few early Christian burial slabs from nearby Saul, where tradition holds the saint began his Irish ministry.

St. Patrick's Well

One of many Irish sacred wells dedicated to the saint, this site north of Waterford features a variety of wells and ruins, along with an early Celtic cross.

Intricate carvings like this one on a stone slab illustrate the Celtic love of elaborate decoration—a characteristic that is also seen in Ireland's wealth of literature and music.

3

Books, Bards, Monks, and Musicians

From ancient mythical superheroes like CuChulain to celebrated twentieth-century writers like novelist James Joyce and poet Seamus Heaney, words and wordsmiths have had a profound impact on Ireland's people, history, and culture.

A Literary Culture

After St. Patrick came to Ireland and began disseminating the Christian message and writing about his experiences, a flood of writing poured forth from Celtic monks, who were some of Ireland's first literary figures, and whose monasteries were a combination of churches and schools. Much of this work was religious in nature, and it included prayers and poems as well as illuminated gospels, of which the Book of Kells is the most impressive surviving example.

Still, the monks who followed in Patrick's footsteps didn't restrict themselves to religious matters. They set about recording the ancient Celtic stories and myths that had been told and retold for centuries but that had never been written down. They also launched a flurry of history writing, compiling annals that would be our first definitive recordings of Ireland's historic growth and development. In addition, the monks made handwritten copies of some of the Western world's best-known works of literature, philosophy, and theology. Little did they know how important these copies would become when the Dark Ages descended upon Europe.

It's relatively easy to record the numerous literary accomplishments of Ireland's Celtic Christian monks. Much more difficult, though, is assessing the impact these lovers of both God and good literature had in launching an Irish literary revolution that continues down to the current day. According to Andrew Greeley, the Chicago priest who may be America's best loved Irish storyteller, Ireland's residents have the highest book consumption rate in the world, and the island has produced "more novelists, poets, storytellers, and playwrights per capita than any other country in the world."

In the pages that follow, we will explore some of the sites that are most closely linked with some of the more important people and works.

Sacred Words

The early Celtic Christian monks devoted themselves to language and learning, but the book they prized above all others was the Bible, and it was upon this sacred book that some of them lavished their most extravagant labors. Sadly, many of the beautiful books the monks created have vanished without a trace—victims of the ravages of time as well as centuries of Viking raids, which commenced during the ninth century. Thankfully, though, one of the monks' supreme works survived, and every year hundreds of thousands of people pay homage to the Book of Kells, which is the subject of an impressive display at Dublin's Trinity University.

The Book of Kells is more than a book. Featuring a dazzling collection of texts from the New Testament Gospels and mesmerizing colorful decorations, it is one of the Western world's most prized masterpieces. It's also a powerful symbol of the blossoming of art and literature that accompanied the rise of Celtic Christianity in Ireland and other lands.

Like a flashy educational video, the Book of Kells was designed to present basic Bible lessons to people for whom literacy was new. More an item of veneration than a document for reading, the book was at once a work of utter devotion to God and a testimony to the near-magical properties of the written word. Dozens of intricate illustrations feature books.

The book's masterpieces are the full-page illustrations of Christ, the Virgin Mary and the Christ child, and Gospel writers Matthew, Mark, Luke, and John. Each meticulously crafted page probably required a month or more to execute. Most of the other pages of the book consist of beautiful Irish script surrounded and interwoven with playful drawings of humans and animals, along with the same kind of intertwining abstract geometric patterns and spirals that appear on Celtic crosses and metalwork. There are also numerous angels and Eucharistic chalices, but not everything is biblically inspired. Many of the illustrations show human figures, some contorted into unbelievable yoga-like positions so they can fit into tiny spaces between the text. Some of these figures are shown in humorous poses, pulling each others' legs or beards. There are also numerous rodents, which may indicate that mice were the lonely monks' most common companions. In one illustration, mice are seen carrying communion wafers in their mouths, and in another, a cat is chasing a mouse who is carrying a host.

The Book of Kells demonstrates that the Christian Celts were accomplished artisans, and that their conversion to Christianity led to a flourishing of creativity, not an otherworldly disregard for the "secular" arts. It may be hard for us to comprehend the utter glee with which the once pre-literate Celts embraced the written word, but perhaps the following poem, written by an anonymous ninth-century scribe, can help us understand their excitement:

> I and Pangur Ban my cat,
> 'Tis a like task we are at:
> Hunting mice is his delight,
> Hunting words I sit all night.
>
> Better far than praise of men
> 'Tis to sit with book and pen;
> Pangur bears me no ill will,
> He too plies his simple skill.
>
> 'Tis a merry thing to see
> At our tasks how glad are we,
> When at home we sit and find
> Entertainment to our mind.
>
> Oftentimes a mouse will stray
> In the hero Pangur's way;
> Oftentimes my keen thought set
> Takes a meaning in its net.
>
> 'Gainst the wall he sets his eye
> Full and fierce and sharp and sly;
> 'Gainst the wall of knowledge I
> All my little wisdom try.
>
> When a mouse darts from its den
> O how glad is Pangur then!
> O what gladness do I prove
> When I solve the doubts I love!
>
> So in peace our tasks we ply,
> Pangur Ban, my cat and I;
> In our arts we find our bliss,
> I have mine and he has his.

Practice every day has made
Pangur perfect in his trade;
I get wisdom day and night
Turning darkness into light.

In February 1999, Trinity opened the doors on its new and improved Book of Kells exhibit, whose title, "Turning Darkness Into Light," alludes to this evocative poem. The exhibit features impressive enlargements of pages from the book, other early Christian manuscripts, and displays about life in Ireland during the ninth century, a time when projects like the Book of Kells were undertaken.

Scribes and Scriptoria

Monks began work on the Book of Kells in the scriptorium of the monastery of Iona, an important Christian center founded by Irish monk St. Columba off the western coast of Scotland (see chapter 9). After Viking attacks ravaged the vulnerable island, the community moved to the landlocked monastery of Kells (or Ceanannus Mor in Gaelic). One of the best pictures of what life in a scriptorium was like comes not from the pens of historians and archaeologists, but from novelist Stephen Lawhead, whose sprawling 1996 novel *Byzantium* opens at the Kells monastery. In one scene, the novel's central character, monk Aidan Mac Cainnech, enters the monastery's scriptorium and examines a manuscript that has been the focus of his labors for days:

Laying aside my pen, I sat in the empty room, looking and listening, remembering all that I had learned and practiced in this place. I gazed at the clustered tables, each with its bench, and both worn smooth, the hard, hard oak polished through years of constant use. In this room, everything was well-ordered and precise: vellum leaves lay flat and square, pens were placed at the top right-hand corner of each table,

and inkhorns stood upright in the dirt floor beside each
bench . . .

I saw the scriptorium [as] not a room at all, but a
fortress entire and sufficient unto itself, a rock against the
winds of chaos howling beyond the monastery walls. Order
and harmony reigned here.

Another recent book, Thomas Cahill's delightful 1995 bestseller, *How the Irish Saved Civilization: The Untold Story of Ireland's Heroic Role from the Fall of Rome to the Rise of Medieval
Europe*, makes the compelling argument that the Irish monks'
appearance on the world's cultural stage at a crucial moment
in history allowed them to preserve much of what we now
treasure as the high points of Western civilization. Cahill
writes:

. . . As the Roman Empire fell, as all through Europe
matted, unwashed barbarians descended on the Roman
cities, looting artifacts and burning books, the Irish, who
were just learning to read and write, took up the great labor
of copying all of western literature—everything they could
lay their hands on [and] single-handedly refounded European civilization.

Cahill marvels that the treasures of the world's culture
would be saved by "outlandish oddities from a land so mar-
ginal that the Romans had not bothered to conquer it." Others
have also acknowledged the important contribution of the
Irish monks. Cardinal John Henry Newman called the long-
vanished Celtic monastic libraries "the storehouse of the past
and the birthplace of the future."

From Prayer to Pubs

It's a long way from Ireland's quiet, ancient monasteries to its
bustling, contemporary pubs, but the celebrated and critically

acclaimed Dublin Literary Pub Crawl honors the Celtic love for language and literature while celebrating the Irish people's unique wit and their endless quest for the perfect pint of Guinness.

The Pub Crawl is a two and a half hour walking tour of historic areas of central Dublin led by a group of professional actors who perform excerpts from the works of some of the city's best-known writers. In a city rich in storied drinking spots, many of which are known for their associations with celebrated writers like James Joyce, Patrick Kavanaugh, Brendan Behan, and Sean O'Casey, the Pub Crawl is an entertaining and educational way to spend an evening learning about Dublin's rich literary culture, visiting some of its most famous watering spots, and making new friends along the way. The *Irish Times* praised the crawl as "a kind of rough guide to the cultural, religious and political history of the capital."

Everything begins at the Duke on Duke Street, an area famous for its connections with James Joyce and the author's masterpiece, *Ulysses.* The walk continues through Trinity University, where writers like Jonathan Swift and Bram Stoker studied, and where Oscar Wilde bristled under the school's strict moral guidelines. Along the way, the actor-guides perform portions of Samuel Beckett's *Waiting for Godot* and O'Casey's *Juno and the Paycock.*

The Pub Crawl, which is sponsored by Jameson, a distiller of Irish whisky, isn't for teetotalers, but neither does it blindly endorse drinking and drunkenness. Although the actors gleefully recite some of the more careless quotes of Brendan Behan ("I'm not a writer with a drinking problem; I'm a drinker with a writing problem."), they also mourn the fact that Behan's uncontrolled alcoholism cut short his life and silenced his unique, powerful voice.

If the Pub Crawl whets your thirst for Irish literature, Dublin offers many other opportunities for satisfaction. The James Joyce Center offers its own walking tour of Dublin, this one focusing on the life and work of the man who is perhaps

Dublin's most celebrated writer. There's also the Dublin Writers Museum, which features exhibits, paintings, manuscripts, and mementos of some of the city's best known wordsmiths, including its three Nobel Prize winners: poet Seamus Heaney (1996), playwright Samuel Beckett (1969), and William Butler Yeats (1923).

A Literary Legacy

The Irish people were appreciating powerful prose and honoring those who used words to educate, inspire, or entertain long before Dublin was a city. In prehistoric times, druids and bards were heralding kings, recounting history, encouraging soldiers, entertaining the bored, and lamenting the dead. Part prophets, part singers, part soothsayers, and part paid political spin doctors, druids and bards created the collective myths of their communities and served as conduits through which supernatural wisdom flowed to kings and their people from the pagan Celtic god Ogmios, who was honored as the god of eloquence.

Many scholars have suggested that some of the more creative bards shifted effortlessly between singing the praises of a tribe's soldiers or king and creating the larger-than-life superheroes who populate much of ancient Celtic mythology. One of the most famous mythical heroes was CuChulain, who wielded a powerful spear that could inflict a fatal blow on his enemies. He was even more famous for a maneuver called the salmon leap, a gravity-defying move that sent him soaring over seemingly insurmountable physical obstacles. Descriptions of some of CuChulain's battles were full of Technicolor gore and bosom-heaving romance. Blood spurted from his head, his body contorted in unusual shapes, and he was occasionally surrounded by naked women. One of his biggest challenges was his battle with a club-carrying giant. He killed the giant and was proclaimed the supreme champion of Ulster.

Victory may have inspired CuChulain, but it was tragedy that moved Amairgin, a member of the Milesians, mythical warriors who came to Ireland from Egypt and Spain. After the death of his wife, named Scene the Shapely, Amairgin was overcome with emotion. He sang the following song:

> I am a wind on the sea,
> I am a wave of the ocean,
> I am the roar of the sea,
> I am an ox of seven exiles,
> I am a hawk on a cliff,
> I am a tear of the sun,
> I am a turning in a maze,
> I am a boar in valour,
> I am a salmon in a pool,
> I am a lake on a plain,
> I am a dispensing power,
> I am a spirit of skillful gift,
> I am a grass-blade giving decay to the earth,
> I am a creative god giving inspiration.

And that was just the first stanza! Following verses included a variety of questions and ruminations on natural and supernatural phenomena, as well as a spell which was designed to encourage fish to swim into the harbor "like a torrent of birds."

One scholar said legends like these represent "the earliest voices from the dawn of Western civilization." They were passed from bard to bard for centuries, until some of them were recorded by Christian monks and scribes. Centuries later, the Irish still love a good yarn, and they honor anyone who can tell one.

Honoring the Eloquent

Many Irish sites pay respect to the eloquence of the islanders. In a sense, that's the allure of Blarney Castle, a popular (and we think vastly overrated) site in County Cork which was built in the mid-fifteenth century. Today the castle is best

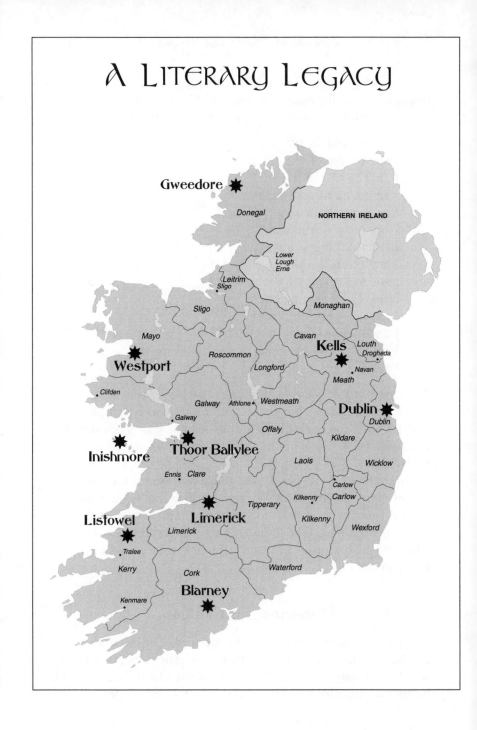

A Literary Legacy

Gweedore

Donegal

NORTHERN IRELAND

Lower
Lough
Erne

Leitrim
Sligo

Sligo

Monaghan

Mayo

Cavan

Kells

Louth
Drogheda

Westport

Roscommon

Longford

Navan

Meath

Clifden

Galway

Athlone

Westmeath

Dublin

Galway

Offaly

Dublin

Inishmore

Thoor Ballylee

Kildare

Ennis

Clare

Laois

Wicklow

Carlow

Listowel

Limerick

Tipperary

Kilkenny

Carlow

Limerick

Kilkenny

Wexford

Tralee

Kerry

Cork

Waterford

Kenmare

Blarney

known for its Stone of Eloquence, better known as the Blarney Stone. Every year thousands of visitors contort their bodies and suspend their usual personal hygiene requirements to kiss the stone, which, according to tradition, is believed to bestow the gift of eloquence.

There are many other places where one can pay homage to the Celtic gift of eloquence. They include:

Limerick

The 1996 Pulitzer Prize for literature was awarded to Limerick-born memoirist Frank McCourt, author of the best-selling *Angela's Ashes*. More recently, McCourt has written a sequel, *'Tis*, but it's the earlier book that won McCourt the Pulitzer Prize (and inspired a Hollywood film). The book is a sad, touching, and humorous account of growing up amid Ireland's grinding poverty. As he writes near the beginning of the book: "It was, of course, a miserable childhood. . . . Worse than the ordinary miserable childhood is the miserable Irish childhood, and worse yet is the miserable Irish Catholic childhood." At first, residents of Limerick weren't sure what to do about McCourt's book, which portrayed their city in an unflattering light. But success has brought a measure of reconciliation, and now visitors can take a tour of McCourt's Limerick. Failing that, they can rent a copy of the video documentary, *The McCourts of Limerick*, which is both touching and sad.

The Aran Islands

Millions of American students have read Irish playwright John Millington Synge's *Riders to the Sea* (1904), a tragic tale of the men who live and die at the whim of the oceans. Synge was living in France before William Butler Yeats challenged him to return to Ireland: "Go to the Aran Islands and live there as if you were one of the people themselves; express a life that has never found expression." From 1898 to 1902

Synge did just that, spending part of every summer on the island of Inishmaan, where he captured the rustic Gaelic speech of the local people. In 1907 he published his insightful study *The Aran Islands*. His most acclaimed work is *Playboy of the Western World*, and his *Deirdre of the Sorrows* is a masterful retelling of ancient Celtic myths.

Listowel

Every June, this pleasant town in County Kerry hosts its annual festival of writing, which celebrates its 29th year in 2001. There are events for adults and children covering fiction, drama, poetry, art, storytelling, comedy, and more. For information, check out the festival Web site (www.kerry web.ie) or send an e-mail (writers@tinet.ie).

Yeats: His Ireland and His Faeries

William Butler Yeats (1865–1939) did more than persuade Synge to return to Ireland: he inspired a whole generation of Irish writers and thinkers to take a deeper look at their roots, spurring a revival of interest in Gaelic culture, arts, literature, legends, and language. A poet, playwright, and ardent Irish nationalist, Yeats also fought for Irish independence.

Yeats is associated with many Irish sites. He was born in Dublin, spent many holidays in County Sligo, and was buried in Drumcliff. His work also features many allusions to Irish sites, including Coole Park in County Galway ("The Wild Swans at Coole"); Parke's Castle in County Leitrim (the setting for "The Lake Isle of Innisfree"); and the western mountains ("Under Ben Bulben"). But Yeats is most closely associated with Thoor Ballylee, a restored castle in County Galway that was his home for seven years.

The love of art and learning continues at Kenny's, a family-owned bookstore and art gallery in Galway.

Yeats was deeply interested and involved in the occult, a facet of this complex man that led writer Stephen Brown to call him "a latter-day pagan." Yeats rejected orthodox religion, and instead studied and experimented with a variety of esoteric practices: he married a medium and spiritualist, joining her in trances and automatic writing sessions; he was a disciple of Madame Blavatsky, founder of the Theosophical Society; and also spent time in London with Aleister Crowley, the celebrated black magic "priest" and author of books on magic and the occult.

Yeats's eclectic beliefs provided him with both a philosophy for life and a system of symbols that he used in his plays *(Pur-*

gatory) and poems ("Byzantium," "Leda and the Swan," etc.).

Yeats's beliefs are explained more clearly in his prose works, such as "The Celtic Twilight," in which he describes a personal encounter he had with faeries from the otherworld, described as "nations of gay creatures, having no souls; nothing in their bright bodies but a mouthful of sweet air."

According to Yeats, during his twenty-seventh year he went to the Rosses, an area of County Donegal renowned for its otherworldly activity. There, as he writes:

> I made a magical circle & invoked the fairies. . . . Once there was a great sound as of little people cheering and stamping with their feet away in the heart of the rock. The queen of the troop came then—I could see her—& held a long conversation with us & finally wrote in the sand 'be careful & do not seek to know much about us.'

Yeats's book *Fairy Tales of Ireland* includes nearly two dozen legends he gathered during his travels. In some of the stories, the fairies are kindly and gentle. In others, they play despicable tricks on their human victims.

Every year for the last forty years, Yeats is honored with an international summer school devoted to drama and poetry. For information, consult the school's Web site (www.itsligo.ie/yeats/yeats.html).

The Song in Their Hearts

Irish writers have long been known for their eloquence, but in recent years it has been Irish musicians who have attracted a growing international audience to all things Celtic. *Riverdance*, the high-stepping Irish music and dance revue, was one of the biggest worldwide pop culture sensations of the 1990s and, along with *Lord of the Dance*, its sequel, has brought greater attention to the richness and depth of traditional Irish culture.

Fans of Celtic music struggle to explain how it seems to sneak up on them and reel them in, but many musicians believe the music's power to move comes from its connections to the mythology, history, and spirituality of the ancient Celtic people.

Dagda, whose name means "good god," was one of the most important pagan Celtic deities. With his harp he could create music that subdued powerful enemies and entranced mere mortals. Dagda's melodies were believed to be vehicles through which flowed a mythical music called "Oran Mor," or creation's all-embracing melody. Tradition says some musicians are granted superhuman understanding of the cosmos and are able to create music that harmonizes with the celestial spheres. Other musicians were said to have been taken away by faeries, who exchanged tunes with them and endowed them with otherworldly musical abilities.

Not everyone remembers these legends today, but most people know that in Ireland the harp remains a potent symbol of Irish culture, and is featured prominently on the country's currency and postage stamps.

The Celtic Christian tradition, which also emphasizes the spiritual power of song, honors the seventh-century poet and musician Caedmon, whose dramatic story was told by early English historian the Venerable Bede.

Caedmon was a simple man with a complex problem: he lived in a music-loving Celtic culture but couldn't sing a note. He was so insecure about his problem that one night, while attending a feast where neighbor after neighbor joined in the riotous song, Caedmon fled before it was his turn to sing and fell asleep in the stable where he cared for a villager's horses. There he had a dream in which a man called out to him and asked him to sing a song.

"What should I sing about?" asked Caedmon.

"Sing about the Creation of all things," the man answered. Caedmon immediately began to sing verses—in praise of God the Creator—that he had never heard before:

Praise we the Fashioner now of Heaven's fabric,
The majesty of his might and his mind's wisdom,
Work of the world-warden, worker of all wonders,
How he the Lord of Glory everlasting,
Wrought first for the race of men Heaven as a rooftree,
Then made the Middle East to be their mansion.

Caedmon, who is memorialized by a cross at the English monastery of Whitby, composed many songs, but these six lines recorded by Bede are the only ones to survive.

For the last few decades, the Chieftains have been traditional Irish music's undisputed ambassadors to the world, creating an impressive body of work totaling more than three dozen albums. In the early 1960s, Irish composer Sean O'Riada founded the groundbreaking Dublin group Ceoltoiri Cualann, which brought new life to old standards. Band member Paddy Moloney left to form his own group, the Chieftains, in 1963. Since then they've played thousands of concerts around the globe, introducing any who would listen to the magic of Irish music. The band plays often in Dublin, Belfast, and other Irish cities, often in pubs featuring traditional Irish musicians. Dublin alone has nearly eight hundred pubs, some of which are featured in the city's Musical Pub Crawl, and many of these feature live music.

One of Ireland's best known music pubs is Matt Molloy's in Westport, on Ireland's western coast. The proprietor (or publican) is Molloy, the Chieftains' flutist. When the band isn't out touring, Molloy occasionally stops by at the pub to play.

Even more off the beaten track is tiny Gweedore in beautiful County Donegal. Perched on the edge of the northwestern corner of Ireland, the isolated, Gaelic-speaking town of Gweedore is home to Leo's Tavern, a small pub that has had a large role in introducing Celtic music to the non-Irish world. It was in this pub in the 1960s that Leo Brennan's children and other relatives first publicly performed their unique mix of traditional and contemporary music. By 1970, they were calling themselves Clannad (which means "a family from the townland of Dore") and winning talent contests. This was just the beginning of a lengthy and ongoing career that would yield nearly twenty albums, including the Grammy-winning *Landmarks* (1998) and would also launch the solo careers of singers Maire Brennan and her better known sister, who goes by the name Enya, and has sold millions of recordings overflowing with melodic, haunting Celtic-inspired music. Leo, who is seventy-six now, still sings at the pub, accompanying himself on accordion. Gweedore is also the place where another highly acclaimed Celtic band named Altan got its start.

In 1996, *Time* magazine said the last decade of the twentieth century had witnessed a "worldwide Irish music renaissance." As a result, Celtic music is increasingly available around the world on CD, radio, in concert, and at festivals. This means that one needn't travel to pubs in remote areas of Ireland to listen to the locals play. On the other hand, there are worse ways to spend one's time.

Little more than an hour south of the hustle and bustle of Dublin, Glendalough overflows with peaceful natural beauty and ancient Christian ruins.

4

Sᴛ. Kevin's Glorious Glendalough

When St. Kevin chose a site for his monastery, he selected one of the most secluded spots in the Wicklow Mountains. Today, hundreds of thousands of people visit Glendalough every year to enjoy its well-preserved sites and stroll its lovely walking trails, which wind through a valley and alongside two lakes.

Saints and Solitude

Although every other chapter in this book covers numerous sites, the present chapter focuses on just one. We've chosen to highlight Glendalough for many reasons, including the fact that we think it's the most beautiful and calming place in Ireland. Beyond that, Glendalough is a powerful way to illustrate one of the recurring ironies of humanity's spiritual experience: that saints and mystics who flee the world to find God in sacred solitude often wind up becoming the center of attention of a throng of devoted followers.

Kevin's Valley

Lonely pilgrims frequently become magnets for others who seek intimacy with God. At least that was the case with Kevin, a gifted man who was born late in the fifth century to Ireland's kingly Dal-Mesincorb tribe. A skilled poet and acclaimed musician, Kevin gave up all his worldly wealth and entitlements and was ordained as a priest, but he didn't seek out a parish to pastor. Instead, he followed a more solitary path: the call to live alone as a hermit in the wild.

Kevin fled to a valley nestled in Ireland's rough and rugged Wicklow Mountains. Ireland is such a green and verdant island that people frequently call it the Emerald Isle, but the Wicklow hills and vales are so luxuriously lush that they have earned the nickname "the garden of Ireland."

Though one of the better known, Kevin was far from the only Celtic saint to seek God in the bosom of nature. Following a pattern established by their pre-Christian predecessors, many early Celtic Christians balanced their devotion to God with a rapturous love for the natural world, which they viewed as the handiwork of the Creator of the cosmos. St. Columba, who is best known for his love of learning, was also enraptured with God's creation, as we can see in the following poem, which he wrote at his island monastery of Iona:

> Delightful I think it to be in the bosom of an isle
> on the crest of a rock,
> that I may see often
> the calm of the sea.

> That I may see its heavy waves
> over the glittering ocean
> as they chant a melody to their Father
> on their eternal course.

The lovely spot Kevin selected for his hermitage was called Glendalough, which means valley of two lakes, but this nature-loving saint didn't spend his days hiking, swimming, or sunbathing. A meditative mystic who practiced a harsh and rigorous life of ascetic discipline, Kevin ate little, slept less, and spent most of his time deep in prayer.

Legend has it that his small dwelling place was a cramped and uncomfortable cavelike cell he carved by hand out of the side of a granite cliff overlooking one of the valley's lakes. Here on the shaded side of the valley only occasionally illuminated by the sun, Kevin prayed, meditated, talked to God, and communed with nature for seven solitary years. One of the saint's biographers describes him as wearing only animal skins and sleeping on a bed of rocks. Another described the otherworldly bliss he experienced in his solitary cell:

> ... The branches and leaves of the trees sometimes sang sweet songs to him, and heavenly music alleviated the severity of his life.

There are many legends from Kevin's biographies illustrating his closeness to the rhythms of nature. One such legend tells how Kevin was close friends with an otter. Once the animal allegedly retrieved the saint's Psalm book from the lake. (Episodes like this are a recurring theme in the biographies of the many Celtic saints who regularly read their Bibles near the water.) The same otter also brought fresh salmon to Kevin.

On one occasion, Kevin was out in the wilderness, fasting and praying to God. As he prayed, a cow approached and licked the saint's feet. That night, the cow produced as much milk as half of the rest of the herd. Day after day, the cow licked Kevin's feet, and night after night it produced an abundance of milk. The herdsman determined to follow the cow so he could find out where she was grazing and take the rest of his cows there. Instead of discovering a miraculous meadow, the man found Kevin, who was weak and feeble because of his fasting. After much protesting from Kevin, the herdsman carried the saint through the woods to a site God had chosen for him to build a church. All along the way, the trees of the forest bent their trunks to give the herdsman room, making it easier for him to carry Kevin to his appointed place.

Another popular legend perfectly captures the essence of Kevin and many other "natural saints." One day, Kevin was deep in prayer, his eyes closed and his arms extended out to his sides with his open palms projecting upward to heaven. While in this position, a blackbird laid an egg in one of the saint's palms. Kevin wasn't disturbed by this visit from one of God's creatures, but continued his prayers as he held the egg in his palm. The saint stayed in earnest prayer, not moving a muscle until a baby bird hatched some many weeks later.

A Gathering Throng

It was only a matter of time before word spread about Kevin's exemplary life of austerity and devotion. Soon the once-solitary saint found himself surrounded by a handful of followers who wanted to learn from him and emulate his life of godly discipline. In time the handful grew into a few dozen. Before long, a small monastic community was being born on a sandy delta formed at a spot where the valley's two rivers met. As one Irish poet expressed it, Kevin "crossed the summits with an angel and built a monastery among the Glens."

Kevin died in 618, and the beloved saint's feast day is still celebrated every June 3 throughout Ireland. His death only increased his renown and the flow of the faithful to the valley.

Before his death, Kevin composed a monastic Rule for his monks. Written in verse, Kevin's Rule governed the daily lives and private devotions of the members of the growing Glendalough community. That Rule is now lost, as are the original buildings Kevin and his brothers built, but other examples of early Celtic monastic Rules have survived, and many of these can be found in the wonderful book *The Celtic Monk*, compiled by twentieth-century Irish monk Uinseann O'Maidin (see chapter 8).

Within years after the saint's death, the dozens of disciples
grew into hundreds, and from the seventh through the
eleventh centuries, Kevin's humble Glendalough evolved into
the center of a large monastic community that housed many
monks and operated chapels, a school, and a farm. As would
happen at other communities throughout the Celtic lands,
Glendalough began to look more like a small, bustling town
than a religious retreat.

Glendalough's evolution from solitary hermitage to busy
monastic community is the story of Celtic monasticism in a
nutshell. In the first few centuries after St. Patrick, Celtic
Christianity didn't grow primarily through churches and
parishes, but through monasteries, which were founded by
devout men and then rapidly became important centers of
learning, spiritual discipleship, and commerce.

Ironically, sites that began as humble saints' lonely sanctuaries became relatively populous and wealthy communities.
Unfortunately, the growing wealth of Ireland's monasteries
made them ripe targets for marauding Viking invaders, who
attacked Christian settlements throughout the island. Glendalough's location in the Wicklow mountains meant that it was
more protected than most, reaching its peak population in the
eleventh and twelfth centuries, a time when many other
Celtic monasteries had closed or were struggling to survive.
By this time, Kevin's once-humble valley housed numerous
churches (the community was long called "Glendalough of the
Seven Churches"), stables, work areas, a water-powered grain
mill, wonderful examples of the unique Celtic crosses and
round towers, and housing for many monks, craftsmen and
their families, and assorted guests.

Glendalough also attracted thousands of pilgrims in the
centuries after Kevin's death. The popularity of making pilgrimages to hallowed and holy sites has waxed and waned
through the centuries of Christian history, but pilgrimages
have always been popular among the Irish. In addition, Ireland attracted pilgrims from other lands who felt safer walking
and praying among the island's Celtic Christians than they did

For centuries, Ireland's kings and saints sought to have their remains buried in Glendalough's holy ground.

among Europe's barbarian invaders, who had plunged the mainland into the Dark Ages. For centuries, Glendalough was one of Ireland's most visited Christian centers.

Kevin's monastery flourished long after many Celtic monasteries had foundered or had been suppressed. It even survived an attack by British soldiers from Dublin in 1398, and monks still lived there until the sixteenth century, when the British government closed down all Ireland's monasteries. The spirit of Glendalough lives on today, as thousands of visitors explore remains of some of the buildings that pilgrims of earlier centuries came so far to see.

Walking Where Pilgrims Walked

There is an impressive visitors center outside the Glendalough monastic complex, located about a mile west of the tiny village of Laragh. The center is often busy and charges a small entrance fee, which you don't have to pay to visit the complex only. However, we recommend stopping there if only briefly. The center houses an exhibition of materials explaining Celtic monasticism and offers a seventeen-minute audiovisual presentation that provides a helpful introduction to Kevin and his popular site.

Visitors enter the monastic complex itself through an impressive stone gatehouse. At one time, most Celtic monasteries were enclosed by walls of stone or dirt. Pilgrims and other guests entered the enclosure through gatehouses like this one. Today, the Glendalough gatehouse is the only such structure to survive at any of Ireland's many monastic communities.

Presiding over the entire complex is a massive round tower which stands over one hundred feet tall. Dozens of ancient and distinctive towers like this one grace Christian sites throughout Ireland, but the one at Glendalough is one of the best preserved on the entire island. Glendalough also features numerous Celtic high crosses, including the impressive St. Kevin's Cross. (For more on round towers and high crosses, see chapter 8.)

The Glendalough complex contains the remains of many church buildings, the most famous and best preserved being St. Kevin's Church. The building is also called St. Kevin's Kitchen because, in addition to its standard stone walls and roof, it features the unique addition of a small round tower as part of the structure, and to some the tower resembles a kitchen's chimney.

Nearby are the remains of St. Kieran's Church. Kieran (also spelled Ciaran) was a monk from Clonmacnois, a monastery in central Ireland. He and Kevin were loving friends and devoted spiritual brothers. So close were these two men that their affection survived death. According to one popular legend, Kevin was on his way to visit Kieran at Clonmacnois when Kieran died. Kevin joined in the prayers for the deceased monk, and it is said that Kieran's resurrected spirit returned to his body and engaged Kevin in a lengthy conversation before returning once again to heaven.

The largest remain in the complex is the roofless Cathedral, and the smallest is the Priest's House (with internal dimensions just under fifteen feet by eight feet). Though small, the house is important. It may have been built to house Kevin's grave and relics. This would explain the building's curious narrow-slit window, which would have allowed pilgrims to view the relics without letting them enter and trample the sacred gravesite. Many local clergy were buried in the area surrounding the house, which is how it got its name. Elsewhere in the complex are many tombs, some of them enclosing the remains of Irish kings. Glendalough and many other Irish monastic sites were long viewed as auspicious places to be buried.

During peak tourist season, Glendalough's ancient remains can seem to be dwarfed by the crush of humanity visiting the popular site. But if the crowds get too big, all one has to do is walk to the nearby foot bridge, cross the slow-moving Glenealo River, and walk the gently sloping, well-maintained path toward the upper lake. Within seconds, the noise of the crowds begins to subside and the solitary joys of Kevin's beautiful valley grow more powerful.

The path provides nice views of the monastery complex and leads to the remains of the Reefert Church, which is about a mile from the main monastic complex. The church presided over a burial ground for many Leinster kings. Nearby are the remains of St. Kevin's Cell, which are believed by some to be the remnants of the hermit's home.

Crossing back over the river, one finds a pathway that winds along the northern edge of the upper lake. From here, one can look back across the lake to view St. Kevin's Bed, a cave carved into the granite walls which is believed to be the primitive cell the saint inhabited for seven years. Beyond the cave is Temple-na-Skelling, or "the church on the rock," which was supposedly built on the same site as the first church constructed by Kevin in the valley. Sir Walter Scott visited and marveled over these sites in 1825, but they are inaccessible today.

The path continues through densely forested land before terminating near the valley's end, where the surrounding mountains rise up hundreds of feet on either side. But walkers wanting a longer trek needn't despair. Back near the east end of the upper lake, the path connects to the famous Wicklow Way, a hiker's dream that begins in Dublin and goes to Clonegal in County Carlow, winding its way for eighty-two miles though some of Ireland's most beautiful countryside.

A Peaceful Valley

We have grown so fond of Kevin's beautiful valley that we often stay there during our first few days in Ireland, saving Dublin for the end of our trip. Getting over jet lag seems easier in Glendalough, and the area is an excellent jumping-off point for many nearby destinations.

Though small, the nearby town of Laragh has just about everything a visitor needs. There is a pub, which serves filling meals all day long, as well as several nice restaurants which serve evening meals. There are numerous comfortable bed-and-breakfasts in the vicinity, as well as a large hotel adjacent to the monastic complex. The area also has a well-supplied woolen outlet featuring a varied selection of Irish sweaters at prices that can be better than those found in nearby Dublin.

County Wicklow also contains numerous sites of interest to students of Celtic history, including the Pipers Stones near

Naas (see chapter 7) and the Baltinglass Burial Mound and Hill Fort.

For many people, the Wicklow Mountains themselves are the main attraction. The Wicklow Mountains National Park contains about fourteen thousand acres of natural beauty. The visitors center for the park is located by Glendalough's upper lake and is accessible by car via the Green Road.

The heart of the area, though, is clearly Kevin's monastery. Those who visit it today can taste a small bit of the natural charm and divine presence that drew the saint to this valley more than thirteen centuries ago. The monastery has been attracting guests and pilgrims ever since. Although the visitors center and main monastic complex can be toured comfortably in a couple of hours, those who really want to appreciate the valley's beguiling beauty should allow a half day or more.

A large family group had all the security they needed in Dunbeg, a sturdy promontory fort with a stunning view located on the Dingle peninsula.

5

Forcresses for Kin and Clan

Dotting the countryside like silent sentinels of a time long gone, Ireland's massive Iron Age forts are stony symbols of both the ancient Celts' heroic past and the bonds and fears that drew them together into tight-knit groups.

Rock-Solid Stronghold

Two and a half millennia ago, those few people who even knew Ireland existed regarded it as a lonely and unimportant outpost on the uttermost edge of the world. Western Ireland, with its rugged coast and equally rugged inhabitants, seemed even more distant and godforsaken. As for Inishmore, the largest of the three rocky Aran Islands located in the Atlantic Ocean twenty-five miles west of Galway, the human mind struggled to comprehend its utter remoteness.

The Iron Age people who inhabited the island didn't see things that way. Their humble homes weren't isolated enough to guarantee their safety, as warring clans and tribes threatened their ancestral lands, their flocks, and their way of life.

63

When efforts to protect themselves proved futile, some of the islanders may have sailed off to seek safety on one of the many smaller islands that surround Ireland's western coast, but most folks dug in, got to work, and began construction on a stronghold called Dun Aengus, which is Ireland's most impressive fort and one of the most impressive building projects of the ancient world.

Choosing their site was easy: a flat, rocky plateau that was the highest place on the seven-mile-long island. In addition to providing commanding views of their surroundings, the site backed up to a sheer, steep cliff that plummeted two hundred breathtaking feet straight down to the Atlantic's pounding waves. Nothing—except perhaps a giant out of the pages of Celtic mythology—could attack the inhabitants from that side!

Attacks from land were much more certain, so the residents began gathering rocks, which then as now are the island's most plentiful resource. With those rocks they began building a series of four massive stone walls which radiated out in D-shaped half-circles from their clifftop perch. The innermost wall, which protected a large area where dozens of members of a clan could gather along with their animals, was twelve feet high and twelve feet thick, and is almost that large today following extensive restoration. The next three walls were shorter and thinner, but each enclosed an increasingly larger area, and consisted of thousands upon thousands of carefully carved and placed stones, the majority of which remain standing today—some 2,500 years after they were erected.

None of these walls would have been totally insurmountable by determined and well-equipped attackers, but the solid stone structures would have slowed invaders down, making them vulnerable to assault from the fort's defenders. Adding to attackers' difficulties were the thousands of small upright stones which were strategically placed between the third and fourth walls. Unlike Ireland's other well known standing stones, which had a clear ritual role, these were purely defensive, and were designed to slow the progress of an approach-

IRON AGE FORTS

ing attacker. Although few of the spikes were sharp enough to draw blood, anyone who tried running through them too quickly risked numerous bruises, or worse. Those who took time to carefully navigate a path through the labyrinth of upright stones were vulnerable to the defenders' arrows or spears.

Irish archaeological expert Peter Harbison calls Dun Aengus "one of the most magnificent and dramatic stone forts of western Europe." Another writer called it "the most magnificent barbaric monument in Europe." Every year it is visited by thousands of curious onlookers and numerous archaeologists.

Dun Aengus isn't the only stone citadel on the Aran Islands, which are a fort lover's paradise. The islands are also home to Doocaher, Doon Farvagh, Dun Conor, Dun Moher, and Dun Onaght, though none is quite as impressive as the massive Dun Aengus.

Still, despite intense scrutiny by international scholars, Dun Aengus remains surrounded by mystery. No one knows precisely who built it, when, or why. What is clear is that it is merely one of an estimated thirty to forty thousand forts that dot Ireland's landscape, most of them probably built by Iron Age Celtic people between 700 B.C. and 700 A.D. These forts stand as mute witnesses to a people and a way of life that long ago vanished from the scene, while at the same time they remain a powerful symbol of one of the strongest links uniting Celtic society—the bonds of kin and clan.

Celtic Family Values

Among the Celts, a clan was a group of people sharing three things in common: ancestors, a family name, and a chief. In prehistoric Ireland, clans were the fundamental building blocks of Celtic society. Larger and more complex than the now-standard nuclear family of father, mother, and children, clans were extended families or kinship groups that consisted of descendants in the male line going back to a common patriarch.

The next largest Celtic social groups were tribes, which were *very* extended families, including hundreds or possibly thousands of people who considered themselves to be of a common ancestry.

Over the centuries, tribes were subsumed into a system of petty chiefdoms. By the time Patrick arrived in Ireland in the fifth century, this system of chiefdoms was giving way to a system of larger, regional royal states, each of which was ruled by a king who controlled many lesser chiefs; Celtic culture of clan and tribe was well on its way to extinction.

The best way to understand what daily life was like among Ireland's early clans is by studying the ancient Celtic myths. Reading these tales, with their vivid portrayals of the celebrated exploits of the Celtic High Kings, one might be tempted to dream longingly of the heroic times they describe, but for those who lived during these turbulent centuries, life could be incredibly brutish, bloody, and brief. Imagine, if you will, living over the hill from a tribe whose fighting men were bigger and perhaps even more flamboyant than contemporary TV wrestlers and you can begin to understand why a tribe would commit itself to the time-consuming and backbreaking work of building a fort like Dun Aengus.

But not all was doom and gloom for the Iron Age Celts. Clans and tribes lived through cycles of calm and chaos. During the good times, families enjoyed relative peace and security that enabled them to raise their children, tend their flocks, and create highly detailed works of Celtic art and jewelry, some of which have survived in all their timeless splendor.

The system of clans and tribes also created a vast social web which provided its members with a strong sense of belonging and identity. Even when they weren't concerned about imminent attack, the Celts were concerned about surviving nature's sometimes vicious ways. The security the tribe offered was comforting, even necessary. There's safety in numbers, and the average Celt was surrounded by dozens, possibly hundreds, of kinsmen and friends. Psychological problems like alienation or anomie were virtually unknown in a society where everyone knew his or her place in the community—physically, socially, and spiritually. As Celtic scholar Nora Chadwick notes, "This tie of the 'kindred' was the strongest of all their early institutions." There were even complex systems of fosterage, which provided for the training and educating of children, and one of the world's first social welfare systems, which ensured that virtually no one would wind up alone and without support.

When times were good, the din of swords and shields faded into the background, and the tribal fort played a mostly symbolic role, projecting an image of the clan's strength and stability to all who could see it for miles around. But when warfare broke out, as it did all too often during those turbulent centuries, the fort became the tribe's cocoon and command center.

Room With a View

The Celts who built Dunbeg Fort, or Dun Beag in Irish, could have built on one of the many local hills, such as nearby Mount Eagle. Instead they chose to build on a narrow finger of land jutting out into Dingle Bay. Like the builders of Dun Aengus, the tribe that constructed Dunbeg depended on cliffs descending to the sea to protect their backs. Unlike Dun Aengus, though, which used tons of rocks for its defensive walls and spikes, Dunbeg had an additional defense: an elaborate series of mounds, ditches, ramparts, tunnels, and trapdoors that would have repelled all but the most brave or stupid of attackers.

We're not sure who built Dunbeg, or from whom they were hiding, but whoever constructed this massive project knew how to foil their human foes. Time, however, and the endless waves of the sea, continue to ravage the fort complex. But even though some of it has fallen into the sea below, Dunbeg remains an impressive edifice situated on an unbelievably beautiful promontory.

The focal point of the whole site is the clochaun, or "beehive" house, which is located near the sea cliffs and was built in the traditional Celtic dry stone manner, without any mortar. Instead of relying on cement, the walls of the house, which are many feet thick, depend on gravity to hold them together. Today, much of the house still stands in its splendid isolation, even if it is ever more precariously close to the sea.

The landward side of the house didn't have the sea to protect it, so its residents constructed a massive stone wall that cuts across the finger of land like a big, gaudy bracelet. Built of carefully stacked stone, the rampart is over twenty feet high and nearly ten feet thick, and extends across the promontory for nearly one hundred feet. A survey taken in the 1850s documented the wall as being twice that long—an indication of the toll erosion has taken over the last century and a half. The side of the rampart facing the house is stair-stepped, so clan members could climb up and position themselves to defend their home. In addition, the one low and narrow passageway through the wall is guarded on either side by hidden chambers, from which a defender could plunge a spear or shoot an arrow at intruders.

Outside the rampart the tiny peninsula widens, and here one can see the complex series of earthen ditches and banks which gave the tribe inside additional protection. There are five lines of ditches, called fosses, which range from three to five feet deep and are between twenty and forty feet wide. Between the five rows of fosses are four rows of banks, approximately three feet high and ten feet wide. These banks and fosses wouldn't have prevented determined marauders from getting close to the stone ramparts, but they would have slowed the invaders down, making them vulnerable to attack from defenders of the fort.

Excavations of the site have turned up some tantalizing information. For example, we know the house was inhabited as early as 580 B.C., and as late as the tenth or eleventh centuries A.D. Holes in the earth indicate that inhabitants once erected tripod stands out of trees, from which they probably hung cooking pots over large fires. Throughout the house area are remnants from meals of mutton, pork, and fish. There's also evidence of an underground hiding chamber, or souterrain, where residents could squirrel away belongings—and themselves—if their defenses were breached.

Variations on a Theme

There are as many different kinds of Celtic forts as there are varieties of pre-Celtic monolithic tombs. The Iron Age Celtic builders didn't follow strict design guidelines, but rather adapted a few general principles to their immediate needs and environments.

Certainly, one of the most unusual adaptations is Doon Fort, which was constructed on a small island in Doon Lough, near the town of Naran in northwestern County Donegal. Structurally, the fort is like many others, with its massive stone walls rising nearly fifteen feet into the air. What is unique, however, is the fort's setting. Situated on a tiny island in a lake, the fort occupies a good 95 percent of the island's land mass. The maximum diameter inside the stone walls, which aren't circular in design but conform to the island's shape, is approximately one hundred feet. Outside the walls, there are places where only a few feet of land stand between the fort and the waters of the lake. Ferrying tons of stone out to the island would have been a Herculean task, but once completed, this fort would have given its unknown builders a formidable defense against anyone silly enough to attempt to cross the lake and attack them.

Much more common, though, were circular hill forts. Instead of relying on water to protect them, most Iron Age Celts found a high hill and began building. Most of the hundreds of Irish hill forts consisted of a circular stone wall with a deep earthen ditch surrounding it. About fifty known examples of the hill fort survive in Ireland. Two of these have been

County Kerry's Staigue Fort is nestled in a valley ringed by mountains, fed by a nearby stream, and provides stunning views of nearby waters.

lovingly restored, and today they are among the most frequently visited forts in Ireland.

One of the most impressive examples of the ancient builders' art is Staigue Fort, near Castlecove, County Kerry, which is easily reachable from the main Ring of Kerry road. The fort is under the protection of the Office of Public Works, but lies on private grazing land. At a gate near the fort, a small box collects donations to the land's owner to make up for trampling on his land and scattering his sheep.

The people who built Staigue Fort had fine taste for site selection. Situated at the top of a beautiful valley, the fort is encircled by rocky green mountains and offers a panoramic view overlooking the Kenmare River and Kenmare Bay. Two nearby streams bring running water to the site.

The fort itself is truly massive, with walls that are eighteen feet high and thirteen feet thick. Visitors enter the circular fort through a short door capped with lintels made of large stone slabs. Once inside the enclosure, which is ninety feet in diameter, you'll notice a number of X-shaped designs that line the inner wall. Upon closer inspection, the designs reveal themselves to be stone stairsteps, allowing one to climb up from the enclosure floor to the top of the walls. In addition, the builders placed a number of small chambers inside the wall at ground level. These chambers could have served as areas for food storage.

Nearly 250 miles north of Staigue Fort and just three miles west of Londonderry stands Grianan of Aileach, which may be the best restored and most propitiously situated of all of Ireland's forts. If ascending to the fort's lofty location doesn't take your breath away, its view—which overlooks Londonderry and parts of County Donegal—will.

Grianan is the Gaelic word for "sunny place," and when the sun is shining, the view from the fort is truly stunning. Aileach is the title that was given to leaders of the O'Loughlin clan, which once ruled the area. Most historians assume the fort was used primarily for defensive purposes, but there are some hints that it may have played a role in Celtic rituals as well, and Celtic myths suggest the circular structure was built by a race of superhuman beings known as the Dagda.

As with Ireland's many other forts, each of which was built in a unique way but which provided essential protection to members of kin and clan, the Grianan's true origins remain shrouded in prehistory.

The Ties That Blind

Just as every family suffers its share of storms and conflict, the Celts' commitment to a clan-based society caused problems, both then and now.

The Celts were rapidly expanding throughout Europe in

the centuries before Christ, thanks in part to their metal swords and fighting bravado. The world was theirs for the taking, but they apparently didn't even try to create a lasting empire. Why?

Historians have puzzled over the fact that the once-dominant Celts were soon forced into the fringes of Europe, from whence they sailed to the British Isles, where they were again, before long, forced to the fringes of Wales, Scotland, and remote Ireland. Why didn't they make a bid for empire? John O'Riordain says the Celts were simple country people whose closeness to the land and their own family roots yielded a localized emphasis rather than a quest for empire. "Their primary interest seems to have been human relations and living in the here and now," writes O'Riordain.

Some would say that the Celts' traditional devotion to kin and clan and their habitual shortsightedness has contributed to the Troubles, which have enveloped parts of Northern Ireland in violence and tension for three decades. Since 1969, more than three thousand people have been killed in the sectarian violence, and thousands more have been injured.

In recent years, the violence has decreased, and calls for reconciliation and negotiation have made significant progress. But anyone who wants things to progress much further will be required to contend with the ghosts of the ancient Celts' tribalism, a force that long ago inspired the building of Ireland's impressive ancient stone forts, but that today may serve as a roadblock to community and cooperation.

Visitors sit among ancient beehive monastic structures and listen to a guide describing the rich history of the rocky island called Skellig Michael, which is located eight miles off Ireland's southwest tip in the stormy Atlantic.

6

Divine Outposts

Mystics have always sought silence and solitude, but the Celtic monks pursued their splendid isolation in a unique way: fleeing to dozens of remote monastic islands. Today, the remains of many of these spiritual outposts provide visitors with a tangible experience of the lives of some of the Celtic saints.

Deserts in the Sea

St. Tola wasn't the most important Celtic saint, but the County Clare site where he founded a monastery, named Dysert O'Dea, is well worth a visit, even though it isn't at the top of our list of important sites. Understanding this place and its unusual name provides insight into the flowering of early Celtic Christian monasticism in the centuries after St. Patrick.

Most people are initially confused when they learn that *dysert* is Gaelic for "desert." They wonder how any place as green and lush as Ireland could have a site named for sun and sand. In addition to Dysert O'Dea, which is named after the seventeenth-century man who helped restore the site, Ireland boasts sites like Dysert in County Limerick, Dysart and

Dysart Tola in County Westmeath, and Dysart Gallen and Dysartenos in County Leix.

The answer isn't found in physical geography but in spiritual history. Christian monasticism was born in the deserts of Egypt, Palestine, and Syria in the first few centuries after Christ. Antony of Egypt, a solitary hermit who fled to the desert to pray and battle Satan, attracted other hermits who settled near him and created the first monasteries in the early fourth century. Antony's *Life,* written by a disciple named Athanasius, helped spread his ideas around the world.

Early Celtic monks devoured Antony's teachings and sought to pattern their lives after his, imitating his devotion to prayer, fasting, and asceticism. When they founded their communities, however, these Celtic Christians didn't have Antony's barren sand, so they found an alternative setting. Ireland is surrounded by water, and its land is divided by flowing rivers and marked by numerous lakes (or loughs), with many of these watery areas featuring islands.

In the sixth, seventh and eighth centuries, holy men and hermits fled to these islands, founding dozens of island monasteries. They provided isolation from the hustle and bustle of daily life and plentiful natural beauty, which the monks viewed as the handiwork of the Creator and valued as an aid to prayer and devotion. The monks established numerous divine outposts throughout Ireland, with nearly a dozen of these named either Church Island or Holy Island. The names of many others began with the Gaelic prefixes "inis" or "inish" (for island), such as Inisfallen in County Kerry's Lough Leane; Inishcaltra in Kerry's Lough Derg; Inishglora and Inishkea North in County Mayo; Inishkeen in County Monaghan; and both Inishtooskert and Inishvickillane off the Dingle Peninsula of County Kerry.

Unfortunately, their isolation made the island monasteries vulnerable to Viking attacks during the ninth and tenth centuries. During this period, many monks were killed, monas-

ISLANDS OF SOLITUDE

teries were laid waste, and important manuscripts were destroyed. Those monks who survived often left their islands to set up communities on the mainland. But after the Vikings' ransacking, pillaging, and burning was done, it was the islands' isolation that helped preserve the remains that were left. As a result, these islands are home to some of Ireland's most outstanding remains, offering visitors wonderful opportunities to step into a different world and get a taste for what monastic life might have been like.

Many regions of Ireland offer a chance to visit an ancient monastic island, but the most impressive and haunting island of them all is an unlikely pinnacle sitting all alone amidst the crashing waves of the Atlantic.

A Holy Haven

The monks who founded the remote and mysterious monastery of Skellig Michael wanted to make sure that their community would be a safe haven for their most important priorities: silence and solitude. To do this, they needed to find a spot where their meditations on God wouldn't be interrupted, either by curious visitors or by the trappings of the world. They wanted to be alone and otherworldly, which was becoming increasingly difficult at some of the mainland Irish monasteries, many of which were evolving into hubs for bustling monastic cities.

Tradition tells us that Skellig Michael (the name combining the Irish word for rock with the name of the archangel believed to bless high places) was founded by St. Finan sometime between the sixth and eighth centuries. When this single-minded monk chose a site for his monastery, he selected one of the most inaccessible, most inhospitable, most amazing sites the world has ever known: a steep, rocky island eight miles out in the Atlantic off County Kerry's southwestern tip.

Then as now, wind and waves can render the island totally inaccessible for weeks at a time. This can be frustrating for the modern-day tourist. We've had many of our attempts to reach the island foiled when locals—like Des Lavelle, the acknowledged living expert on the island's history, folklore, and wildlife—refuse to offer boat trips to the site when huge ocean swells make landing on the island impossible. One time, we did manage make it to the island, but the journey was terrifying, the landing was treacherous, and the wind— which caused raindrops to speed horizontally so they hit us in the face like tiny bullets—made it impossible to fully appreciate the island's beauty, although it did increase our respect for the place's hardy former inhabitants.

Much of the time, Skellig Michael, which sits where the Atlantic's Gulf Stream approaches the rocky coast of Ireland, is wracked by winds and battered by waves that have gathered strength during their two-thousand-mile journey from the waters off Newfoundland. But the very conditions that can frustrate today's visitors gave security to the Celtic monks whose quest for silence and solitude took them to a place writer George Bernard Shaw said possesses a "magic that takes you out, far out, of this time and this world."

The community that made the rock their home was never a large one. From the time monks first inhabited the island in the centuries after St. Patrick to the time they relocated to a mainland Kerry monastery called Ballinskelligs in the twelfth century, there were probably never more than a dozen or so men. We don't know much about the monks who made their home on this rocky refuge. Although the island receives a few mentions in early Irish annals, no written records created on the island itself have survived, which isn't surprising. Beginning in the 820s, Viking raiders sacked the island, and they would continue to do so on and off for much of the next three centuries. Even if it weren't for human invaders, the harshness of the elements could have easily destroyed any of the monks' vellum or parchment books. Des Lavelle says that in 1951 wind and waves broke the lantern glass of the island's old lighthouse, which stood 175 feet above the sea below.

Years later, waves destroyed a sturdy steel gate, washing it to the bottom of the ocean, where Lavelle found it and brought it up. Today the mangled gate is featured in a display at the Skellig Experience Center, which is securely located on the Irish mainland.

The monks spent many hours of every day in prayer and devotion. Much of the rest of their time was occupied in trying to eke out a living from their harsh environment. While Skellig Michael does have forty-four acres of land, little of the island is level enough for gardens or crops, and researchers have concluded that the monks couldn't have grown enough food to sustain themselves. They did have a few sheep and goats, but there were no cows or pigs, which probably would have slipped off the island's steep, rocky cliffs into the swirling ocean below. During much of the year, the monks most likely dined on fish, birds, and birds' eggs, all of which were in plentiful supply. They probably bartered their surpluses of these products with mainlanders for vellum, grain, firewood, and other necessities.

A brief tour of the island also makes it clear that the monks devoted considerable time and energy to creating a beautiful, sacred space on the barren, inhospitable rock.

Their amazing monastic complex was located some 550 feet above sea level. The site has been carefully restored by the Irish parks system and features half a dozen drystone "bee-hive" huts, all of which were originally constructed without mortar by the monks, who spent years selecting and delicately placing the stones. All of these round buildings have conical roofs and plenty of space inside. In each, two monks would have lived, slept, studied, and prayed. In addition, there are two larger oratories shaped like overturned boats. Here, the brothers gathered for corporate prayer and worship.

The monastery is situated in a small area of the island which faces the mainland and is therefore protected from some of the Atlantic's fiercest gales. The complex is surrounded by as many stone walls as the terrain allows, and there are terraces designed to prohibit the monastery and the soil it stands on from slipping downward into the sea.

But how did the monks get up to their sacred perch? Three separate pathways lead from sea level to the monastery. All three routes include extremely steep stretches, many of them featuring solid stone steps that, like the monastery itself, were crafted by the monks. Lavelle says there are some 2,300 of these stone steps on the island.

Ironically, the island's inhospitality and inaccessibility have helped preserve the monastery's ancient remains, making Skellig Michael, one of the world's best-preserved examples of early Christian architecture. Every year, an estimated 12,000 to 15,000 people ride boats out to visit the island. The parks employees who manage the site say that more would come if the seas weren't so rough, and if the island itself wasn't such a tough place to visit: There are no restaurants, rest rooms, or elevators.

Its relative inaccessibility makes visiting the island even more of a thrill for those who succeed in reaching it. Over the centuries, many who have made the trek have documented their reactions to the site in journals, stories, and songs. More than a century ago, British adventurer Lord Dunraven visited Skellig Michael and remarked on the site's "sense of solitude," with "the vast heaven above and the sublime monotonous motion of the sea beneath." More recently, musician Loreena McKennitt included a song entitled "Skellig" on her bestselling 1997 recording *The Book of Secrets*.

Prior to 1992, those who were unable to reach the island left the area disappointed. Now, an attractive new visitors center offers the next best thing: an informative film, detailed displays, a shop full of books and mementos, and a small dining room. In addition, the center offers a much calmer boat trip that circles the island but does not land. For many, the center and its excursion are as near as they will ever get to this ancient and majestic monument to monastic silence and solitude.

Islands of Calm

Some people think monks are aloof, alien beings who care little for the world and the people in it. Most of the monks and mystics we know, however, are deeply concerned about all these things; they simply care more about spending time alone in prayer and devotion to God, and they organize their lives in such a way that this priority isn't squeezed out of their schedules by the mundane cares of daily life.

Today, most of us inhabit an environment that is noisy, flashy, and sensation saturated. When we're not bombarded by the mass media, we're surrounded by the noise of people, traffic, cell phones, lawn mowers, boom boxes, and other sonic assaults which conspire to make our lives more chaotic and less reflective.

The Celtic monks who fled to Ireland's monastic islands some twelve centuries ago didn't have to deal with the kinds of noise we regularly encounter, but they did struggle with the deeper issue of choosing what would take priority in their lives. For these religious radicals, there was no question that drawing closer to God was their primary purpose. As a result, they ran to silence as to a long-lost friend, finding there the embrace of God, along with a tremendous sense of inner peace and tranquillity.

Contrast the chaos of modern daily life to the calm portrayed by the tenth-century Celtic monk who wrote these lines:

. . . . I have a hut in the wood, no one knows it but my Lord; an ash tree this side, a hazel on the other, a great tree on a mound encloses it. . . .

The size of my hut, small yet not small, a place of familiar paths. . .

A little hidden lowly hut, which owns the path-filled forest; will you go with me to see it? . . .

In summer with its pleasant, abundant mantle, with good-tasting savor, there are pignuts, wild marjoram, the cresses of the stream—green purity! . . .

The swarms of the bright-breasted ring-doves . . . the carol
of the thrush, pleasant and familiar above my house . . .

Swarms of bees, beetles, soft music of the world, a gentle
humming . . .

A nimble singer, the combative brown wren from the
hazel bough . . .

Fair white birds come, cranes, seagulls, the sea sings to
them, no mournful music . . .

A beautiful pine makes music to me, it is not hired;
through Christ, I fare no worse at any time than you do.

Though you delight in your own enjoyments, greater
than all wealth, for my part I am grateful for what is given
me from my dear Christ.

Without an hour of quarrel, without the noise of strife
which disturbs you, grateful to the Prince who gives every
good to me in my hut . . .

Reading this passage, it's easy to sense the calmness and cen-
teredness that resonate from each word. This monk wasn't
alone in his deep love for creation and the Creator. Many of
the surviving literary works composed by Celtic monks
express similar sentiments.

The people who wrote lines like these and built monasteries like Skellig Michael weren't antisocial introverts fleeing
the world for their own personal comfort. Rather, they were
humble disciples trying to carve out a space for God in their
lives.

Uinseann O'Maidin is a modern-day monk who lives at
Mount Melleray Abbey in County Waterford. His excellent
book *The Celtic Monk* is a collection of monastic rules, many of
which focused on the important issue of silence—both exter-
nal and internal. The Rule of Ailbe, which was probably written down sometime during the eighth century, devotes much
attention to outlining how a monk could maintain a meditative
quiet. "Two-thirds of piety consists in being silent," states the
rule, before instructing the monk in the best ways for achiev-
ing such quietude:

Let his work be silently done, without speech. Let him not be garrulous, but rather a man of few words. . . . Be silent and peaceful, that your devotion might be fruitful.

Now, centuries after these words were written and Ireland's Celtic monasteries were built, the monks' search for stillness of soul and calmness of surroundings speaks volumes to us about our own noisy lives.

Island Hopping

The Celtic monks built few monasteries on Ireland's eastern and southern shores, where their isolation might have been interrupted by people sailing between England and Scotland or from mainland Europe. Most of the Celts' island monasteries were situated in remote inland lakes or out in the ocean off Ireland's rugged western coast, where there was nothing to bother the brothers but waves, wind, birds, and fish. Or, as Kenneth Hurlstone Jackson writes in his collection *A Celtic Miscellany,* "The Celtic hermits went to the most desolate wilds and ocean rocks to win salvation in their own way . . ."

Many of the islands that once housed monks and monasteries are accessible to today's visitor, especially in the best of weather. Two of the more rewarding and most accessible islands—Inishmurray and Inishbofin—are located less than one hundred miles from each other off Ireland's western coast.

Inishmurray is a small (223 acres), low-lying (its highest point is seventy feet above sea level) island located four miles off the County Sligo coast but reachable, weather permitting, from the town of Mullaghmore.

Its monastery was probably founded by St. Molaise, who lived during the sixth century. By the year 802, the Vikings had made their first attacks, but there were still monks on the island into the twelfth century. Surprisingly, even after the monks left, the island remained inhabited for centuries, perhaps originally by some of the monks' relatives. The island's population was never large. Patrick Heraughty, who was born on the island and lived there until he was twelve, writes that "at its height in 1880, Inishmurray boasted a population of 102." A community numbering a few dozen souls lived on the island until it was finally abandoned in 1948 due to unforeseen financial circumstances. (Heraughty writes that the island's soil was never very good, and that getting freshly caught fish to mainland markets quickly was always a challenge, so most islanders survived by making illegal whiskey. Irish law enforcement officials made many unsuccessful attempts to stamp out the whiskey trade, which failed only after World War II and the onset of sugar rationing.)

Some of the islanders' humble houses can still be seen, most of them much worse for wear than when they were vacated just over half a century ago, but that's not what makes this island so important. Rather, it's the survival of many of the ancient monastic remains that are. Inishmurray's main claim to fame. Archaeology expert Peter Harbison says the island is home to "the most striking medieval complex anywhere in Ireland."

From a distance, the site's most impressive feature is the huge, thirteen-foot-high stone wall—and, in some places, the wall is nearly that wide—that surrounds the main monastic complex. It's as if the island's monks had applied the Iron Age Celts' fort-building techniques to creating their own circular sacred space. Inside the main enclosure are shorter walls which subdivide the area into smaller compartments, and it is here that one finds the substantial remains of a church, a smaller oratory building, a wonderfully restored beehive hut, and some carved burial slabs.

Outside the massive walls one finds numerous unique stone monuments, many of which were part of the monks' stations of the cross. The sixteen stone stations, each of which is creatively carved, cover a fairly large area. Heraughty writes that the people who lived on the island in the twentieth century routinely walked the stations. As part of an annual religious festival, islanders recited prescribed prayers and performed traditional rituals during a procession around the stations which took three to four hours to complete.

If a visit to Inishmurray is like stepping back in time, going to Inishbofin Island is like entering a time machine and rapidly passing through the last *five millennia* of Irish history. Reachable by ferry from Cleggan, a coastal town in western Ireland's beautiful Connemara region, Inishbofin (the name means "island of the white cow," and comes from ancient legends) is relatively small, but it has the remains of megalithic tombs, Iron Age forts, a seventh-century monastery, and a thirteenth-century abbey. But the site that towers over all the rest is Cromwell's Barracks, a large, star-shaped structure built by British soldiers in the seventeenth century. Hiking and climbing trails provide easy access to all the sites, or you can rent a bike. There are also options for lodging and dining.

Other Outposts

There are a number of other Celtic monastic islands which are easier to reach and nearly as interesting.

Inishmore, Aran Islands

Some say that St. Enda's monastery, which once flourished toward the southern end of the largest of the three Aran Islands, is where Irish monasticism was born. Enda, who lived during the fifth and sixth centuries, was a renowned teacher, and among his many pupils were some of the most celebrated Celtic saints, including Columba, Brendan the Navigator, and Finan of Clonard. Time and tide haven't been kind to Enda's monastery, which vanished centuries ago, but the site is now home to the remains of a small chapel and a graveyard.

St. Enda set up his monastery on the coast of Inishmore. Today, a chapel and a graveyard grace the spot.

Nendrum Monastery, Mahee Island, Strangford Lough, County Down

Possibly one of Ireland's oldest island monasteries, Nendrum is said to have been founded by St. Mochaoi, who, according to tradition, was converted to Christianity by St. Patrick, and who died before the year 500.

In addition to its age, Nendrum might well be the most thoroughly excavated of all the early Irish monasteries. There are stone walls, remains of buildings, decorative stones, and a nice interpretive center that attempts to explain the site in historical context. Nendrum is reachable by car over a narrow winding causeway.

Lower Lough Erne, County Fermanagh

Three intriguing island monasteries can be found within a few short miles on this lake north of Enniskillen.

Devenish Island, one and one-half miles north of Enniskillen, is the most impressive of the three. The site of a monastery said to have been founded in the sixth century by St. Molaise has a nice round tower that visitors can climb, the remains of a thirteenth-century church, and a museum. Like the other sites on the lake, the monastery also features some intriguing stone carvings that are unlike those found anywhere else in Ireland. In season, boats regularly go to the island from Trory Point.

Both Boa Island, which is reachable by car, and White Island, which is reachable by boat from the Castle Archdale marina, are known for their unique and mysterious carvings. Some, such as the series of carvings found on White Island, are clearly Christian in nature. Archaeologists are less sure about at least one of the stones on Boa Island, and can't decide if it has Christian or pagan origins. Either way, these small island monasteries show that art, and possibly other traditions, developed along often highly individual lines at the different divine outposts.

Scattery Island, County Clare

Scattery is a small island located in the estuary of the River Shannon, south of the town of Kilrush. St. Senan is said to have established a monastery here. Senan, a student of St. Ciaran, reportedly died in 544, making this one of the earlier Irish monasteries. It withstood attacks from Viking invaders, English plunderers, and Norman soldiers, surviving into the sixteenth century. Also surviving are a unique round tower (its door is at ground level, while all other Irish round towers have an elevated entrance) and other remains.

Tory Island, County Donegal

Legend says that this monastery, located eight miles off Ireland's northwestern corner, was founded by St. Columba. The island, which is still inhabited, doesn't feature extensive remains, but one can find partial remains of two churches and a round tower. More interesting is an unusual T-shaped cross. An additional note: Tory Island was long an important stopping point for Irish musicians, who visited the islanders in order to learn some of the old songs.

Visiting one of Ireland's monastic islands requires planning and the cooperation of natural forces, but the effort is well worth it.

Photographs, rosaries, candles, and stones represent prayers uttered at this holy well, located on the island of Inishmore.

7

High Places and Thin Places

The ancient pagan Celts believed that the physical world was bathed in a numinous spiritual aura. This belief led to a deep love for the land and the creation of hundreds of sacred spaces and shrines, many of which can be visited today.

Portals to the Otherworld

Whether they know it or not, most Westerners are disciples of Plato, the Greek philosopher who drew a solid line between body and soul, separating earthly, physical existence from the transcendent, eternal realm of ideas, or forms. The roots of the belief system of the ancient Celtic people, however, were in the East, where sages stressed unity, not duality, and saw the world and everything in it in terms of oneness and harmony, not atomization and discontinuity.

The Celts who migrated to Ireland were pagan pantheists who believed that supernatural forces pervade the natural world. Instead of following one God believed to be the creator of the cosmos, the pre-Christian Celts worshipped a pantheon of gods and goddesses, many of whom were associated with the deceased ancestors of a specific clan or tribe, or were identified with a particular local geographical feature, such as a nearby hill or stream.

Although they subscribed to the view that the gods were everywhere and in all things, the Celts also believed that certain physical sites were "thin places," or open portals between the worlds. At these thin places, which could be natural sites like hilltops and holy wells, or human-made features like sacred stone circles, the gods and the spirits of the dead mingled with the living in most powerful ways.

Over the centuries, many of the pagan thin places were appropriated by early Celtic Christians, who built churches for worshipping God on some of the same sites that had previously been used for pagan rituals. Information about many other ancient sacred places has vanished without a trace. However, hundreds of Celtic thin places can be seen today, giving the visitor a unique understanding of some of humanity's earliest religious impulses.

High and Holy

In the hilly area of County Kerry near Killarney there are two huge earth mounds reaching nearly 700 feet into the air. They resemble women's breasts, but size and shape are only part of why locals call them the Paps. Their full name, in Irish, is An Da Chich Danann, or in English, the Paps of Anu. To the ancient Celts, who viewed the earth as their mother, the peaks were seen as the breasts of the goddess Anu, who was believed to be the source of fertility and fruitfulness, and whose name appears on natural features all over the Celtic landscape, as well as in town names, like Annan in Scotland.

For pagan Celts, the Paps and other hilltops and high places were sacred sites, but for centuries, none of these high places was more sacred than the Hill of Tara, both an important ritual site and the seat of the High Kings of Ireland.

Mystical Places

Donegal

NORTHERN IRELAND

Lower
Lough
Erne

Leitrim
Sligo

Monaghan

Tobernalt well
Sligo

Mayo

Cavan

Louth
Drogheda

• Westport

Roscommon

Hill of Tara

Longford

• Clifden

Athlone   Westmeath

Navan fort
Meath

Kildare   Dublin
Dublin

• Galway

Galway   Offaly

Dun Aillinne

Inishmore

Laois   **Piper's Stones**
Wicklow

Clare

Ennis •

• Carlow
Carlow

Kilkenny •

Kilkenny

• Limerick

Tipperary

Kilkenny

Wexford

Limerick

• Tralee

Kerry   Cork

Waterford

The Paps

Kenmare stone circle

Drombeg stone circle

Located north of Dublin in County Meath, Tara has been an important spiritual site since at least 2000 B.C. Around that time, pre-Celtic Stone Age people built a passage tomb on the hilltop to house their dead. Centuries later, the hill became an important royal site. At first, Tara was the seat of one local king, but later the king who ruled from here was hailed as the most powerful in all of Ireland.

A significant amount of mythology has grown up around the history of the Celtic kings, particularly Arthur, who was a historical person about whom very little is known. Some scholars believe it is likely that Arthur ruled over a small sixth-century kingdom, possibly in Wales, that he was mortally wounded in battle, and that he was taken to Glastonbury, England, where he died.

By 1469, when Sir Thomas Malory finished *Le Morte d'Arthur*, Arthur's simple biography had been gloriously transformed. The Arthur of fifteenth-century fiction was a chivalrous Christian king who ruled over a large kingdom. More recently, Marion Zimmer Bradley's 1982 novel *The Mists of Avalon* imagines what things would have been like for the women of Arthur's time.

Leaving legend aside for the historical facts about Ireland's Celtic kings, we know that there may have been hundreds of kings or chieftains ruling over "kingdoms" as small as a few hundred people or as large as ten thousand or more. Most of these kings were pagans who were hailed as demigods and were believed to serve as important intermediaries between this world and the otherworld. As Celtic scholar Liam de Paor put it, kings served as a kind of communal guardians, providing both physical and spiritual care:

> . . . to protect a pastoral and agricultural people against the arbitrary forces of nature, such as drought, storm, famine, lightning and disease, imagined as malevolent interventions by divinities or otherworld beings.

The less important kings owed allegiance to one of many more powerful provincial kings, each of whom owed ultimate allegiance to a ruler known as the High King. For centuries, the most important and legendary of Ireland's High Kings ruled from Tara. During this time, Tara was home to a number of large wooden ceremonial buildings, all of which are long gone.

Although Tara is just slightly over five hundred feet tall, it provides a commanding view of the surrounding countryside, including views of the Hill of Slane where, in 433 A.D., St. Patrick lit a Christian bonfire to compete with Tara's pagan fires (see chapter 2). In the centuries after Patrick, however, Tara's importance waned. Today all that's left of those glory days are numerous earthworks spreading out over the hill and its environs. The best view of the complex is from the air, but studying a map or an aerial photo of the site before visiting will give you an adequate appreciation for what you're seeing.

The dominant feature of the hill today is the so-called Royal Enclosure (all names are from the Middle Ages, and may not accurately reflect the ways ancient people used the site). Inside this ancient circular ditch and mound are some of Tara's most important monuments, including the Mound of the Hostages (the name given to the Stone Age tomb) and the Stone of Destiny, an upright pillar believed to be related to the coronation of High Kings, or perhaps to ancient fertility rituals.

In the immediate vicinity are a number of other earthen forts and trenches. Nearby stands a statue of St. Patrick that, along with a church located down the hill, reflects the Celtic Christians' earnest desire to stake a claim to important pagan sites. The church now serves as an interpretive center for the hill and its monuments.

Tara was ancient Ireland's most honored high place, but it wasn't the only one. Two miles west of Armagh lie the remains of the once-famous Navan Fort, which was an important spiritual and social site for centuries; so important, historians say, that it was the reason St. Patrick chose nearby Armagh as the seat of the diocese he established. This prehistoric capital of the kingdom of Ulster was one of Ireland's major sites. Today, visitors can stroll the man-made hilltop and explore one of Northern Ireland's most impressive visitors centers, complete with displays, a shop, and a nice restaurant.

West of County Kildare's town of Kilcullen is Dun Aillinne, which was an ancient ritual site before it became the seat of the Kings of Leinster. Once home to many substantial buildings and significant events, now the site is lonely and unremarkable, except for the gorse that grows along its large outer circular enclosure.

Today Tara is undoubtedly the most rewarding of these three sites. Still, those who don't really know what they're looking for, or who expect to see tangible signs of Arthurian-era royalty, may be disappointed by their visit to these once-impressive high places.

Sacred Waters

Many major faiths honor water as sacred, from the Hindus' ritual baths in the sacred Ganges River to the Christians' baptismal font. The pagan Celts revered rivers like the Danube and the Boyne as domains of their goddesses. They also believed that shorelines—where water and land met and intermingled—were sacred junctions where humans could connect more directly with invisible spiritual forces. Ireland, which is subdivided by rivers, dotted by lakes, and surrounded by the sea, offered pagans plenty of watery thin places.

An even more popular place to commune with the deities was near a sacred spring or well. The Celts venerated natural springs, building shrinelike structures around the spots where the cool, clear water emerged from the ground. The Irish weren't the only early people to worship at wells. The practice was common in India and Africa, and the Romans built water

Although it's not on the normal tourist routes, the ancient Drombeg stone circle—one of Ireland's best preserved—attracts visitors who want to experience its mystical aura.

shrines wherever their empire spread. One of the more impressive examples is Bath in southwestern England, which was dedicated to the goddess Sulis Minerva. In some areas of Ireland, the veneration of holy wells continues to the present day, even though most wells are now dedicated to Christian saints rather than pagan deities.

The Celts built shrines around wells, left offerings in their pools, and bathed both newborn children and dying elders in their cool, clear waters. Some wells were believed to contain healing power. In many cases, these wells served as the poor rural people's family doctors, and rocks or clay from around some wells were taken home and used to treat or prevent illnesses. Stone slabs near the wells were used as chairs or couches for people to sit or lie on near these healing waters. Examining some of these slabs today, one can see how they have been worn down after centuries of visits by the faithful.

One of the best-known Celtic holy wells is in the Welsh town of Holywell, and is dedicated to St. Winefride, a saintly woman who, according to legend, had her head cut off for refusing to have sex with a stranger who was passing through the area. A spring of fresh water appeared at the very spot where her head fell to the ground.

No one knows how many holy wells there are in Ireland, but a recent book says nearly one hundred can be located in a small area of southern County Louth. Patrick Logan, author of the 1980 book *The Holy Wells of Ireland* says his research revealed that Ireland is home to thousands of sacred wells.

One could spend a lifetime trying to find and visit all of these sites. Instead, here is brief list of some of the most impressive and oldest.

- Logan's book mentions more than a dozen wells dedicated to St. Patrick, one of which is located on the grounds of Trinity College, Dublin, underneath the Nassau Street Entrance. Legend says that when Patrick visited the area, locals told him the water in their well was brackish. The saint prayed and the water was purified. (There are nearly one hundred other wells in County Dublin.)

- Wells dedicated to St. Brigid are as numerous as those dedicated to Patrick. Two of the most important are located in Liscannor, County Clare and Mullingar, County Westmeath.

- The well at Tobernalt (which means "cliff well"), three miles south of Sligo, has a long and varied history. In preChristian times, it was a pagan site, later becoming a Christian site. During the eighteenth century, a time when England was enforcing oppressive restrictions on Ireland's Catholics, priests came to the well for clandestine celebrations of the Mass. In addition to the well itself, which remains a place of pilgrimage, one can still see the rock that was used as an altar.

- On Inishmore, the largest of the Aran islands, there is an attractive well located behind the remains of the fifteenth-century Teampall an Cheathrair Alainn, which is Gaelic for "chapel of the comely saints." Both the chapel and the well are dedicated to four saints popular on the island: Fursey, Conall, Berchan, and Brendan of Birr. An examination of the well reveals that it remains an important site of devotion.

Visiting sacred wells is relatively easy, for they can be found in almost every area of the country. Visitors should be respectful of those who may be praying there. Visiting a well that's off the beaten path, you may observe people practicing ancient rituals and circling the wells; and visiting on the feast day of a well's patron saint may mean competing with dozens of others to get near the water, because many wells are small and humble. But if you take a moment to examine the rocks, relics, and mementos left by people who have prayed at these sites, you will realize that they don't seem small at all to people of big faith.

Sacred Stones

In 1997 Paul McCartney received a series of thunderous standing ovations. The applause wasn't for one of the former Beatle's pop hits, but for his latest composition, a classical oratorio entitled *Standing Stone*. Over the course of seventy-five minutes, McCartney's sprawling orchestral work charts early human history and expresses the composer's fascination with the prehistoric people who erected huge upright stones throughout much of Europe.

A few years earlier, bestselling writer F. Scott Peck's unusual memoir *In Search of Stones* describes the lasting allure of some of England's massive monoliths:

> ... during ... one of my previous youthful trips to England, I was on a train to visit some friends and by pure chance got to see a long row of standing stones in a field outside the fast-moving window. I wished I could have somehow

stopped the train and gotten out to hug them. The sight had haunted me ever since. It had stayed so vividly in my memory I'd even wondered whether it might not have been a dream.

Millennia ago, pagan people created and then abandoned thousands of evocative stone installations, hundreds of which still stand in places as diverse as Almendras, Portugal; Carnac, France; and England's Stonehenge and Avebury sites. No matter where they stand, these stones serve as silent reminders of ancient people and mysterious practices long vanished from the Earth.

Ireland doesn't have anything as elaborate as these celebrated sites, but it does have many fine standing stones, stone alignments, and stone circles. One of the most celebrated Irish stone circles is located near the country's southern coast.

Drombeg ("the small ridge") is the name archaeologists have given the circle west of the town of Roscarberry, County Cork, which was probably built in the centuries before the time of Christ. There are a number of stone circles in the county, and they have anywhere from five to nineteen stones. The Drombeg circle, which sits on a pleasant hillside and has a clear view of the nearby ocean, consists of seventeen stones. Most of the stones are the same height, including the two so-called "portal" stones; and one lies flat. Some scholars believe Drombeg is an astronomical site, and that the rays of the rising sun shone through the portal stones to illuminate the flat stone, but no one is sure precisely how the stones were used.

The circle did play some kind of ritual role, though. Excavators found at least one cremated body within the circle. The stones also seem to have served as the centerpiece of either a small community or a seasonal hunting place. Just west of the circle are the remains of two connected huts and a cooking area, which had an ancient roasting oven as well as a large water trough. Stones found near the trough were heated in a fire and then dropped into the water, bringing the water to near-boiling temperatures almost instantly.

Northwest of Drombeg lies a somewhat smaller stone circle, but its location outside the charming town of Kenmare, County Kerry, makes it exceedingly easy to find and visit.

Much more difficult to find is a County Wicklow circle known as the Piper's Stones. There are signs south of Hollywood directing visitors to the stones, but that's merely where the fun begins. We searched through two cow pastures before finding the circle in a third field. Unfortunately, the legend surrounding the circle—that a musician and his listeners were turned to stone for dancing on the Sabbath—is more interesting than the circle itself, which consists of irregularly shaped boulders, some of them decorated with cow dung. Even the enthusiastic F. Scott Peck would have stopped short of hugging these stones.

Still, even a circle like the Piper's Stones can amaze and mystify. We may never know all we would like to about when these many monuments of stone and earth were built, or by whom, or for what. In the meantime, at least we can imagine.

Naming the Land

For centuries, pagan Celts inhabited Ireland's hills and vales and lived along its rivers and coasts. In many ways, their relationship to the land was much deeper than ours. While we may drive our cars through a landscape and remark on its beauty, the Celts felt a strong bond to the land, a bond that was heightened by their belief that the land's high places and thin places harbored beneficial spiritual blessings and powers.

As the Celts migrated from Asia through Europe to Ireland, they left their cultural imprint on the land through the names they assigned to it. From London, which the Celts called the "fortress of Lugh" after one of their pagan deities; to the Danube River, originally named after the Celtic goddess Danu; to Paris, which was named after the Parisii, a migrating Celtic group, their impact reached far and wide.

Today, the visitor can gain insights about ancient sites by unlocking the meaning of their names, a process made easier by books on the subject, which one can purchase at Irish book shops.

For example, the town of Red Hill, located near Skreen, was formerly called Knocknadrooa, which means "hill of the druids." More than sixty Irish place names begin with some variation of the word *knock*, which is Irish for "hill," including Knockatober ("the hill of the well") and Knockaderry ("the hill of the oak wood").

Over time, the early Celts' pantheistic paganism gradually came to be replaced by Christianity. The Celtic Christians kept the love of the land alive, even though they did so for different theological reasons than their pagan predecessors. The Celtic Christians were monotheists who saw divinity in God alone. In their view, the thing that made a hilltop or a coastline sacred wasn't any inherent divinity of the land itself, but was rather derived from nature's relationship to God, whom St. Patrick called "the Creator of all Creation."

Christian theology speaks of the transcendence of God, which can sometimes make God seem aloof or removed, but the Christian faith also speaks of the immanence—or closeness—of God. Columba, the founder of the Scottish island monastery of Iona, spoke of this immanence of God in one of his sermons:

> Yet of his being who shall be able to speak? Of how He is everywhere present and invisible, or of how He fills heaven and earth and every creature, according to that saying, Do I not fill heaven and earth?

More recently, writer Andrew Greeley created this winsome prayer of blessing, which also expresses God's immanence: "May you be as close to God as God is to you."

As Christian churches began to be erected across Ireland, often on hills that had once been pagan ritual centers, the

Irish prefix *kil-* (which means "church") began popping up in many place names. There were towns located near churches dedicated to particular saints or holy men and women, such as Kilbeggan ("Beccan's church") or Kilcolman ("St. Colman's church"). Other place names explain the church's surroundings, such as Kilcullen ("church of the holly") or Kilfithmone ("the church of the wood of the bog"). In addition to names honoring Irish saints, there are more than fifty places named Kilmurry, or "church of the Virgin Mary."

But the mother of all Irish place names is attached to a little village on the island of Anglesey which has the world's second longest place name: Llanfairpwllgwyngyllgogerychwyrndrobwllllantysiliogogogoch. It means "Church of Mary near the white-hazelnut spring near the wild maelstrom by the Sysitischapel in the red cave."

No matter what they are called, though, Ireland's many sacred sites continue to move and mystify nearly anyone who visits them.

Monks carved elaborate stone Celtic crosses like this one at Monasterboice, which features panels illustrating numerous biblical scenes.

8

Cities of God

Ireland's early Celtic monasteries and its later European-influenced abbeys came from two distinct periods of Irish history, but their goals were the same: to provide havens for those who wanted to learn about and meditate on the ways of God.

Centers for the Soul

All major faiths have both an outer expression, which is concerned primarily with public rituals and social ministries, and an inner dimension, which is intensely focused on invisible things of the spirit and the soul.

The Christianity that blossomed in Ireland during the first few centuries after St. Patrick emphasized the inner dimensions of the faith. Many pagan Celts converted to Christianity, but Ireland did not immediately sprout numerous large, impressive churches. Instead, the faith spread mainly through humble monasteries, where believers devoted themselves to prayer, study, and a deepening spiritual growth.

Some of the earliest Celtic monasteries were founded in the fifth century, but we have almost no physical remains from

any of these centers of the soul, many of which were constructed out of timbers, straw, and mud daub. More substantial
buildings were erected during the sixth, seventh, and eighth
centuries, and it was also during this period that monks began
carving the many beautiful Celtic crosses which have become
such a powerful symbol of the Celts' unique brand of Christianity. But during the ninth century, much of this progress
was severely challenged as Viking raiders damaged or
destroyed Celtic monastic buildings and massacred many
monks. The most powerful monuments to these troublesome
times are the tall and stately Irish round towers, which were
built to protect the monks and their possessions. Many of
these round towers still stand over monastic sites today.

Many monasteries never recovered from the hard times,
and even those which did survive saw the fervor of their
monks begin to wane. In the twelfth century, an Irish monk
named St. Malachy helped lead a monastic revival, and in
1140 he sent Irish monks to Clairvaux, France, to study at the
Cistercian monastery there. Two years later, a group of monks
who had studied at Clairvaux returned to Ireland to found
Mellifont Abbey north of Dublin. In succeeding centuries
waves of European-trained monks came to Ireland, opening a
brand-new period of Ireland's monastic history. Cistercian,
Augustinian, Carmelite, Dominican, and Franciscan monks
built numerous impressive European-style buildings, often on
the sites where earlier Celtic monasteries had been based.
The remains visitors see around Ireland today date largely
from this later period.

Previous chapters have examined Kevin's beautiful Glendalough monastery site, as well as a number of monastic
islands. In the pages that follow, we will explore a few more of
the important early Celtic monastic sites, as well as some of
the later abbeys. Along the way, we'll take a look at Ireland's
unique Celtic crosses and monastic round towers.

Our coverage won't be exhaustive, nor could it be. One
map of monastic Ireland, published by an Irish government

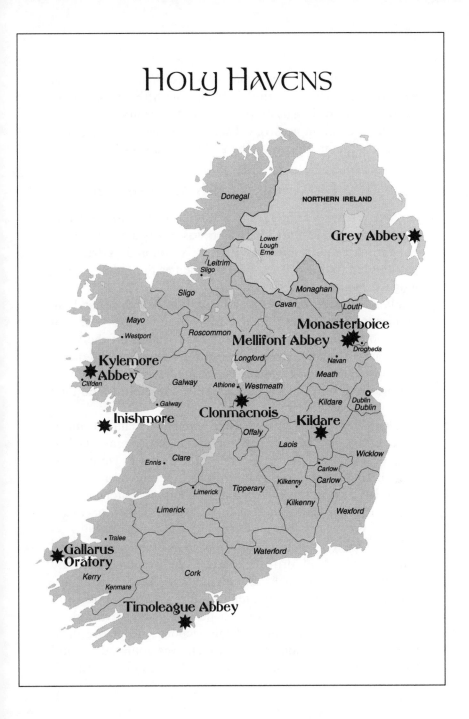

agency in 1959, included more than one thousand sites that were in existence some time between the fifth and sixteenth centuries. We will focus on those sites that are most rewarding to visit, offer an impressive collection of remains, and have an important role in Ireland's long and unusual history.

The Flowering of Irish Monasticism

No one knows when St. Enda was born, but he probably died some time around 530, which was nearly a century after St. Patrick came to Ireland. Patrick is honored as Ireland's patron saint, but it is Enda who is hailed as the father of Irish monasticism.

Many scholars believe that Enda founded the first Irish monastery around 484 on the rugged and rocky island of Inishmore, the largest of the three Aran Islands off the western coast of Ireland. Enda received the islands from Aengus, King of Cashel, and the saint established a small community that was known for its harsh rules, severe discipline, and total separation from the world.

There's no evidence that Enda sought out fame or influence, but before he died, his small, isolated community had become a beacon of monasticism for the rest of Ireland. At his school, Enda instructed many of the men and women who would later found some of the most important centers, including Brendan of Clonfert, Finian of Clonard, Jarlath of Tuam, and others.

Today there's not much left of Enda's original monastery. Shifting tides and drifting sands have washed away any remains of his original settlement. But the beautiful bay where he once prayed and taught is now a quiet and peaceful site featuring the remains of a chapel and small graveyard.

Enda's legacy lives on at Clonmacnois, one of the most renowned Celtic monasteries, which was founded around 545 A.D. by a monk named Ciaran, who was one of Enda's best-known disciples. His master had been content to teach and pray on the outermost edge of Europe, but Ciaran established his monastery in the middle of Ireland, right at the intersection of the country's busiest roadway and major river trade route.

Ciaran was an unusual man who combined an intense inward-looking spiritual depth with an expansive outward-looking evangelistic vision. He could spend days alone in prayer and mystical contemplation, but he also went out on evangelistic journeys, enthusiastically promoting the Christian message and the monastic lifestyle. Unfortunately, Ciaran died of the yellow plague at the age of thirty-three, only seven months after founding Clonmacnois. Still, the vision he instilled in his disciples made the monastery one of Ireland's important Christian centers.

Geography played an important part in the monastery's considerable influence. Nearly all roads led to Clonmacnois, which is located roughly midway between Dublin and Galway and just south of the present-day town of Athlone. The site is on the banks of the River Shannon, Ireland's longest river, which was then a major north-south water route. The site is also on the border between two Celtic kingdoms, which meant Ciaran could draw support from both without being beholden to either. In addition, Ciaran's chosen location straddled the island's most important east-west overland route: a roadway following the course of an ancient chariot path which ran along a natural ridge.

Over the years, many of Ireland's kings prayed at Clonmacnois, and some of their graves are on the grounds. The monastery also developed a renowned school which housed a large library. Some of the world's best scholars taught there, and the community's residents created early histories of Ireland as well as The Book of the Dun Cow, a collection of secular texts. In addition, some of the period's most accomplished stone carvers worked at Clonmacnois, creating dozens of huge

Celtic crosses. The Cross of the Scriptures and the South Cross feature elaborate carvings of biblical personalities and scenes, and stand more than twelve feet tall. The North Cross features an unusual carving of a cross-legged figure some say might be the Celtic god Cernunnos. Most of Clonmacnois's weather-beaten crosses have been moved into the protection of the adjacent visitors center, which offers tours, a video, and materials about the site.

In some ways, visiting Clonmacnois feels like stepping back into Ireland's distant past. Long gone are the simple wooden churches and huts that would have been built during the monastery's early days. Instead, one sees a tall round tower which was probably built during the tenth century and the remains of numerous buildings built mostly during the twelfth and thirteenth centuries and expanded or repaired during later centuries. One additional building is a good bit newer than that: it's a shelter that was built to cover Pope John Paul II, who held a well-attended papal Mass here in 1979.

Brigid

Elsewhere in Ireland, other monastic sites are affiliated with the monks who founded them, including Ita of Limerick, Finian of Moville, Comgall of Bangor, Mobi of Glasnevin, Brona of Clonbroney, and Maedoc of Ferns. One of the more interesting monastery founders, and one of Ireland's most beloved saints, is Brigid of Kildare.

We really know very little about this popular saint, whose name graces more monuments and churches than even Saint Patrick's. There's a lack of solid historical material, but to make matters more complicated, Brigid's biography has been mixed with folklore, legend, myth, and miracle so that the real Brigid is lost in a cloud of confusing and often contradictory stories.

She might have been baptized by Patrick, and she probably died around 525. No one knows when she was born, but her feast day is celebrated on February 1, the same date of the ancient pagan holiday of Imbolc, which celebrated the coming of spring after a long, cold winter. Perhaps more than any other saint, Brigid's legend is intertwined with pagan myths and spiritual practices. In fact, hers is the name of an earlier pagan goddess of fire and song. In addition, Brigid's famous monastery in Kildare was called Church of the Oak, although it's not clear whether the church was named after a nearby tree or whether there was some deeper association with a pagan shrine that Brigid Christianized.

What made Brigid's center most unusual was that it was founded as a "double" monastery with facilities for both men and women. Thus Kildare was a powerful symbol of the Celtic Christians' radical egalitarianism. Regarded as one of the most important monasteries of the Celtic church, Kildare trained numerous monks and nuns, many of whom went on to found their own centers.

So strong was the devotion to this saint that faithful followers kept a fire burning in her honor at Kildare for more than a thousand years. The oppressive English regime finally extinguished the flame when it shut down all of Ireland's monasteries following the Reformation, but the zealous affection the Irish feel for this saintly woman has not died down.

Today, the beautiful St. Brigid's Cathedral, which was built during the thirteenth century, is well worth a visit, and the nearby monastic round tower provides anyone willing to climb its many steps with a panoramic view of the charming town of Kildare.

When one visits places like Kildare and Clonmacnois today, it's hard to imagine what the daily life of an early Celtic monk or nun would have been like, but the rules that were written at many of the monasteries can give us a good idea.

A Quiet Joy

Celtic monasteries weren't sad, sorrowful places. Rather, they were characterized by a calm, quiet joy, as we can see from this rhapsodic description of communal Christian life found in the Rule of the Grey Monks.

> A melodious bell, pealing out over the glen, such is the will of the fair Lord, that many brothers may be gathered under one discipline.

The Rule of Cormac Mac Ciolionain is equally upbeat:

> Happy the moment when I hear of a stable community, one not given to chatter. The melodious chant of the believers is as food to me . . .

Many of the monastic rules collected by contemporary monk Uinseann O'Maidin in his informative book *The Celtic Monk* express the communities' goals and the individual members' primary responsibilities:

> In this lies the heart of the rule: to love Christ, to shun wealth, to remain close to the heavenly king, and to be gentle towards all people.

We know that many monasteries practiced a form of spiritual discipline known as soul friendship, a term that comes from the Irish term "anam cara" and means "one who shares my cell." Most Celtic soul friends did room together, but they shared much more than a common dwelling. They prayed together, they encouraged each other, and they confessed their sins to each other, a practice that some believe helped inspire the more formal style of confession that is still practiced today in the Roman Catholic church.

Typically, soul friendship involved an older monk, who served as a spiritual guide, and a younger monk, who was a pupil of the master. Some of the monastic Rules, like the Rule of Carthage, contained sections which spelled out the duties and obligations of spiritual guides:

> If you are a spiritual director to a man, do not barter his soul; be not as the blind leading the blind; do not leave him in neglect . . .
> Pay their dues of fasting and prayer; if not, you will have to pay for the sins of all . . .
> Instruct the unlearned that they may bend to your will. Do not allow them to fall into the path of sin by your example . . .
> Do not be miserly with others for the sake of wealth; your soul is of more value to you than riches. . . .
> Yours is the duty of chanting intercessions at each canonical hour when the bells are rung. . . .

Additional Rules laid out general principles for all the members of a community. Sometimes the Rules stated members' obligations negatively:

> Do not eat until you are hungry.
> Do not sleep until it is necessary.
> Do not speak until necessity demands.

Other Rules expressed things in the positive:

> Each day carries with it three duties: prayer, work, and reading.

Work could involve anything from harvesting crops to milking cows, but we also know that at many monasteries, work involved labors of skill and craft such as manuscript illumination, metalworking, and carving stone crosses.

Celtic High Crosses

Nothing expresses Celtic Christianity as clearly and simply as the beautiful Celtic crosses, which one writer described as "prayers in stone." Pre-Christian Celts had long marked off sacred territory with sacred stones, columns, and monuments. The Christian Celts were no different. At first, Christians in Celtic lands merely carved cross symbols on existing pagan stones. By the eighth century, monastic artists were busy carving distinctive Celtic crosses.

Today, more than a hundred of these crosses survive in Ireland, with many more in Cornwall. No one knows how many crosses there were before many were ravaged by the elements or destroyed by Protestants who believed the crosses represented Catholic idolatry.

The most distinctive element of the cross is the ring that surrounds the crossbeams. Although some researchers argue that the circle was merely an engineering device designed to provide support for the weight of the heavy horizontal beams, there are also persuasive arguments that the ring was primarily a symbolic design element.

Circles were important spiritual symbols to pagan Celts, as we can see from their tombs and stone circles. Perhaps by combining a cross and a circle, the early Celtic Christians were trying to demonstrate that they believed Christ to be the center and culmination of all things. The cross also symbolized Christ's lordship over all of creation.

Artists covered the crosses with extensive, extravagant designs. Some of this design work was abstract and geometrical in style, utilizing the same kind of intricate interlacing that decorated Celtic metalwork as well as the artwork on the pages of the Book of Kells.

In addition to this abstract art, many crosses featured numerous panels that were used to display various biblical characters and scenes. The West Cross at Monasterboice,

County Louth, is Ireland's tallest at more than twenty-one feet, which means it has more room for biblical panels. The front side alone has twelve panels, each crammed full of biblical elements and motifs. Muiredach's Cross, another important Monasterboice cross, is unique because of the detailed inscription on its shaft. This cross is among the best preserved in all of Ireland, making its detailed carving clear and clean.

Clonmacnois has many crosses and partial crosses, and it was believed that this monastic center was the home of a major workshop where sculptors created crosses for other monasteries throughout Ireland. The crosses carved at Clonmacnois are famous for their precise design work.

The Cross of the Scriptures is probably the best known cross at Clonmacnois. Its weatherworn panels tell the story of Christ's Passion, beginning with the events of Palm Sunday and concluding with the Resurrection on Easter Sunday, which takes center stage at the hub of the cross's beams.

For illiterate Celtic believers, carefully carved crosses were a powerful visual method of conveying important theological concepts. For us, they are a graceful reminder of the creative flowering of Celtic Christianity.

Towns and Towers

At most major monasteries, there was more going on than prayer, gardening, and cross carving. Over time, many monasteries evolved into small villages, complete with carpenters' workshops, forges and metalworkers, and communities of workers and relatives that could house a thousand members or more. Only a small percentage of these people would have been monks, whose living quarters and worship areas were kept separate from the communities' more secular concerns.

One place where this evolution can be seen most clearly is at the present-day town of Kells, which grew up around the monastery of the same name. (Until recently, one of the monastery's stone crosses stood in the town square, but after a few run-ins with automobiles, it was moved to a more protective environment.)

In part, it was the growing wealth and affluence of the monastic communities that made them prime targets for Viking raiders, who made their first appearance along Ireland's coasts in the 790s. These raids would continue for the next two centuries, and by the year 1000 there were few monasteries that hadn't been attacked and rebuilt at least once.

It was during the centuries of Viking raids that monks and other workers started building Ireland's unique round towers, of which more than sixty survive today.

The Irish word for these towers was "cloicthech," which meant "bell house" or "bell tower." When it was time to summon monks to prayer, one of their brothers would ascend the monastic round tower, and soon the ringing of the bell could be heard throughout the valley. But these towers were much more than belfries. Standing between seventy to one hundred feet in height, the towers made excellent lookouts as communities tried to protect themselves from Viking invaders.

In most round towers, the lowest opening was a doorway located ten feet off the ground. A wooden ladder was used to reach the doorway, then once the monks were inside, they would take the ladder in with them.

There is also evidence that the towers were made to protect more than the monks. As Celtic monasteries grew in size and wealth, they accumulated possessions that attracted the attention of Viking raiders or even local bandits. The round towers often served as vaults for the monks' manuscripts, which would often be gilded with precious metals or embossed with valuable jewels, as well as the monastery's Eucharistic goblets and instruments, intricately made bells, and other valuable items.

Ireland's abbeys—like Clonmacnois, pictured above—were
once the centers of an influential monastic revival. Today,
sites like Grey Abbey near Belfast are quiet and bucolic.

Round towers also served as beacons for religious pilgrims who sometimes journeyed miles on foot to visit a monastery, receive a blessing from the monks, and touch the sacred bones and holy relics of deceased saints. Some of the round towers could have been seen from miles away by weary, prayerful pilgrims.

Only three of these unique structures can be found outside of Ireland: two are located in Scotland and one is on the Isle of Man, says scholar Peter Harbison. Some of Ireland's towers are in disrepair, but excellent examples can be seen today at Glendalough, Ardmore, Clonmacnois, Devenish Island, and Kildare. The most unusual is the tilting tower at Kilmacduagh, County Galway, which is the Celtic equivalent of Italy's leaning tower of Pisa.

From Monasteries to Abbeys

St. Malachy, the Irish monastic reformer, founded the Cistercian abbey at Mellifont, County Meath, in 1142. St. Bernard of Clairvaux, the founder of the Cistercian movement, had asked Malachy to "search for and prepare a place . . . far removed from the turmoil of the world." This secluded glen alongside the river Mattock seemed like the perfect spot.

During its boom years, Mellifont had three hundred lay brothers, and by the end of the century Ireland was home to more than two dozen Cistercian abbeys, with half a dozen of these being established as daughter houses of Mellifont. One of these daughter houses was Boyle Abbey in County Roscommon, which features a varied mix of architectural styles.

Eight and one-half centuries later, all that's left of Mellifont are portions of a few large buildings and the foundations of a few more. Like many religious houses, sacking by invaders and plundering by neighbors looking for accessible building materials have lessened its former glory.

A more impressive Cistercian monastery is Grey Abbey, which is located in a grassy area west of Belfast at the village of Strangford Lough. Founded in 1193 and built with the help of brothers from England's Lake District, the abbey is the first fully Gothic-style building in Ireland, as one can see from its many arches, windows, and doors, all of which are pointed rather than rounded. A nearby visitors center includes informative displays about the abbey's design and construction as well as the daily life of the monks.

Other fine Cistercian abbeys include Jerpoint Abbey, County Kilkenny, and Baltinglass Abbey, County Wicklow.

Like the Cistercians, who came before them to Ireland, the Augustinians (or more correctly, Canons Regular of St. Augustine) built a number of fine abbeys. Two of the most impressive are Ballintober Abbey and Cong Abbey, both located in County Mayo. A later Augustinian priory built in Fethard, County Tipperary, is still in use today.

Other European monastic groups established centers in Ireland as well, including the Benedictines (Fore Abbey, County Westmeath), the Dominicans (Kilmallock Priory, County Limerick), the Carmelites (Loughrea Friary, County Galway), and, in the thirteenth century, the Franciscans.

The followers of St. Francis built many attractive friaries, including Ennis, County Clare; Muckross, County Kerry; and Slane, County Meath. One of the more interesting Franciscan houses is Timoleague Abbey, located west of Kinsale in County Cork.

Founded in the mid-thirteenth century and continually expanded until it was abandoned around 1630, the abbey was a sprawling complex featuring a chapel, a kitchen, a library, and storerooms. Today, one can stroll through the impressive remains, imagining how life might have been lived here centuries ago. One of the abbey's most attractive features is the friars' dining hall. True to the nature-loving spirit of St. Francis, the hall has five large windows which look out to the calm waters of Courtmacsherry Bay.

Now the natural world has invaded the empty abbey, with birds nesting and vines growing among the walls that once housed the sounds of worship and prayer. Perhaps it was such a forlorn sight that inspired nineteenth-century Irish poet Sean O'Coileain to write his poem "Elegy on the Ruins of Timoleague Abbey," which contained this line: "There was a time when this house was cheerful and glad."

Other Sites

One doesn't have to go far in Ireland to come across an ancient monastic site or the remains of a later abbey. The island is full of religious buildings, including two unique sites that are well worth visiting.

Gallarus Oratory, located in the Dingle Peninsula, County Kerry, is the best remaining example of an unusual form of architecture that was used in a number of religious buildings erected during the sixth, seventh, and eighth centuries in western Ireland. These buildings are frequently called boat-shaped oratories, because from a distance they look like the bottom side of an overturned boat. Upon closer examination, though, Gallarus can be seen for what it is: a carefully crafted drystone structure whose builders lavishly selected, shaped, and placed these stones on top of one another without any mortar. Their excellent work has survived for more than a millennium.

The West's beautiful Connemara is home to many wonderful sights, including Kylemore Abbey, which is one of Ireland's more popular tourist destinations, even though it wasn't originally built as an abbey. Nestled among the Twelve Bens near Clifden in County Galway, the massive Gothic Revival castle was a present from English tycoon Mitchell Henry (1826–1911) to his wife Margaret. After her premature death in 1874, a heartbroken Mitchell sold his dream home, which was later occupied by Benedictine nuns who had fled the horrors of World War I in Belgium. Today, nuns run a girls' school and operate a splendid visitors center, gift shop, and dining room.

Ireland's St. Columba founded the historic monastery of Iona off Scotland's rugged western coast. Today, a vibrant Christian community keeps the Celtic spirit alive on the island.

9

Pilgrims
in Distant Lands

*Celtic monks like Brendan and Columba set out across the
seas in tiny leatherskin boats for unknown destinations far,
far away. Today there's much we can learn from their
joyful approach to wandering the world for God.*

The Love of Travel

One the themes that has continually reappeared in this book
is the Irish people's almost overpowering attachment to their
land, from the ancient pagan Celts with their sacred geogra-
phies and many localized deities, to the Christian Celts with
their seaside monastic outposts where monks could commune
with both creation and the Creator. Now we will examine the
Christian Celts' seemingly inexhaustible urge to travel.

The Celts were amazed by biblical stories about Abraham,
the Jewish patriarch whose life was transformed after God
commanded him: "Leave your country, your people and your
father's household and go to the land I will show you." They
also marveled over Matthew's Gospel, which says that Jesus

was a wanderer who "had nowhere to lay his head." Closer to home, St. Patrick had been a man on the move, from his enslavement in Ireland to his return years later for an itinerant ministry that took him throughout much of the island.

Part of the Celts' desire to move around was inspired by a deep curiosity about the world God had made, something scholar Edward Sellner calls "their innate yearning to explore the unknown." Traveling exposed the Celts to aspects of God's creation they hadn't seen before, and gave them a chance to visit hallowed holy sites and see esteemed saints' relics.

Another aspect of their wanderlust was evangelistic in nature. The Christian Celts believed God had blessed them with two wonderful gifts: a unique understanding of the glories of the faith, and an innate knowledge of seafaring, which came from living on an island crisscrossed by rivers and lakes. The Celts combined theology and geography in unique and intriguing ways, developing a belief in something they called "the place of one's resurrection." This idea held that God called everyone to a specific geographic location where he or she could experience a deeper sense of spiritual presence.

If it hadn't been for their transforming faith in God, the Celts probably would have preferred to stay home. Leaving the land they loved wasn't easy. One writer suggested that in sailing away from home into the vastness of the seas, the Celtic Christians were "crucifying their body on the blue waves." They even had a term for it: White Martyrdom, which they defined as a divine calling to leave all that is known and familiar, to trust in the mercies of God, and to head out into the unknown and often untamed lands. Lisa Bitel, author of *Isle of the Saints*, writes:

> Irish monks deliberately left their homes, kinfolk, and allies to seek sanctity in foreign wastes. They devoutly believed that their deaths in the wasteland . . . would bring spiritual rewards beyond anything they could find at home.

Columban, who was one of the most widely traveled Celtic monks, put it like this:

> Therefore let this principle abide with us, that on the road we so live as travelers, as pilgrims, as guests of the world.

Today, a growing number of travelers seem to be looking for something more than a superficial tourism which glides across the surface of foreign lands. They want a deeper connection to people and places whose rhythms are different from the familiar routines of home. Perhaps by studying the globe-trotting Celts, we can develop a deeper appreciation for the joys to be found in the journey.

The Navigator

The incontrovertible facts of St. Brendan's life are relatively few. He was born sometime around 486 near Tralee in western Ireland's beautiful County Kerry. He studied with St. Enda at the early monastery on Inishmore, the largest of the Aran Islands. He returned to the mainland, traveled, and founded many Christian centers, including Clonfert, which would become one of Ireland's most important monastic schools. He died sometime around 575.

Everything else about this curious saint is subject to intense debate and disagreement. Did he really set out with a group of men to sail the seas for seven years in search of a promised paradise? Did his little boat take him and his men across the ocean to far-away Iceland and North America? And did he truly battle huge sea monsters and have many other amazing experiences en route?

These are just a few of the mind-boggling episodes recorded in *The Voyage of Saint Brendan* (or in Latin, *Navigatio Sancti Brendani Abbatis*), a work that was written in Ireland around 800 and went on to become one of the Middle Ages' biggest literary sensations. Fifteen years before Christopher Columbus sailed to North America in 1492, he visited the Irish city of Galway, where he studied Brendan's journals and maps and recruited a local seaman to help him on his planned Atlantic crossing.

A cross between Homer's *Odyssey*, Bunyan's *The Pilgrim's Progress*, TV's *The X-Files*, and the miracle stories of the New Testament Gospels, *The Voyage of Saint Brendan* is a big, bold tale of spiritual quest and transformation writ large over a background of sun and surf. The hard part is trying to separate history from hagiography, fact from fantasy, and mysticism from maritime adventure.

Legend tells us that Brendan was in church one day when he heard a reading of one of Jesus' more enigmatic sayings:

> ... everyone who has left houses or brothers or sisters or father or mother or children or fields for my sake will receive a hundred times as much and will inherit eternal life.

Brendan took the message to heart and prayed to God for permission to cross the seas in search of the so-called Land of Promise, an Edenic paradise believed to be located in the sea to the west of Ireland's rocky western coast. Soon, an angel appeared to Brendan, saying, "Arise, Brendan, that which thou hast requested thou shall receive of God, and that is to visit the Land of Promise at last."

Brendan then began a series of adventures and misadventures that required two voyages over seven years and are chronicled in *The Voyage*. He and his crew visited St. Enda on the Aran Islands, then proceeded west, where they came upon an island "full of hideous furry mice as large as cats." Next they came to two more amazing animal islands, one full of large, brilliantly white sheep and the other full of many "marvelous" birds. Dangerous water lulled Brendan's men to sleep;

and just when all were growing despondent, "a bird alighted that moment on the prow of the ship, and made music sweet as an organ with its wings, beating them on the sides of the boat." With Easter came time to find land and celebrate the Lord's resurrection. The men alighted on an island that turned out to be a huge, hospitable whale. After Easter, the men resumed their journey and the whale swam away, but the giant creature returned on schedule the next three Easters, allowing Brendan and his crew to celebrate the Eucharist on his body again and again. Finally, after dodging a few dangerous whirlpools, Brendan and company returned to Ireland to tell others about their experiences.

And that was only the first lengthy journey! The second outing included demon dwarfs, nasty metalsmiths who tried to hurl molten metal at their boat, a fight between two sea monsters, a narrow escape from a menacing sea-cat, and a visit to a small island where Judas Iscariot, the betrayer of Christ, lived out his eternal torment.

There's a passage in John J. O'Meara's lively 1976 translation of *The Voyage* which reveals much about the spiritual zeal that animated Brendan and his men. One day after celebrating Mass, the men saw a sky-high pillar floating in the sea and surrounded by a wide-meshed net. Some of the men cautioned against going too close to the mysterious island, but Brendan ventured forth, filled with a childlike curiosity about the world and a saint's faith in the world's sovereign God, telling his monks: "Let the boat in through one of the meshes, so that we can have a close look at the wonders of our creator."

At many points during their seven years at sea, Brendan and his men risked drowning, attacks by various sea monsters, and went for weeks without food or water, but they never gave up hope. Instead, they drew from a deep reservoir of faith in God. So strong was that faith that, at times, they sailed without using oars, sails, or tiller. As Brendan explained: "Is not God the pilot and sailor of our boat? Leave it to him. He Himself guides our journey as he wills."

At last the men found the long-awaited Land of Promise, which was everything they had hoped it would be, and more. Brendan and his mates wondered why it had taken them seven years to find the land of their quest. The explanation was given to them by a youth who greeted them upon their arrival on the island: "You could not find it immediately because God wanted to show you his varied secrets in the great ocean." In other words, getting there wasn't the point; it was all about the journey.

While some scholars have totally dismissed *The Voyage* as a work of medieval fantasy, others have argued that parts of it ring true, or are supported by fact. For example, when the Norwegians "discovered" Iceland in the 800s, they found the remains of Irish books and religious artifacts. Monks had already landed there centuries before.

Until the 1970s, most skeptics loudly proclaimed that it would have been impossible for Brendan and his men to sail to America in one of the Irish monks' tiny leather boats, or coracles. Some of these skeptics changed their tune on June 16, 1977, when seaman and writer Tim Severin guided a Brendan-style coracle into Peckford Island, Newfoundland, after a harrowing but successful ocean crossing. "We made it!" crowed Severin in his 1978 book, *The Brendan Voyage*. "A leather boat that some had feared would disintegrate in the first gale had successfully crossed the Atlantic. There was no longer any practical objection to the idea that Irish monks might have sailed leather boats to America before the Norsemen, and long before Christopher Columbus."

There's still plenty about Brendan and his legend for scholars to debate, but at least Severin put an end to questions about whether one of the Celtic monks' boats could have survived a journey to the New World.

If you would like to experience something of Brendan's life, but you don't feel like crossing the ocean in a coracle,

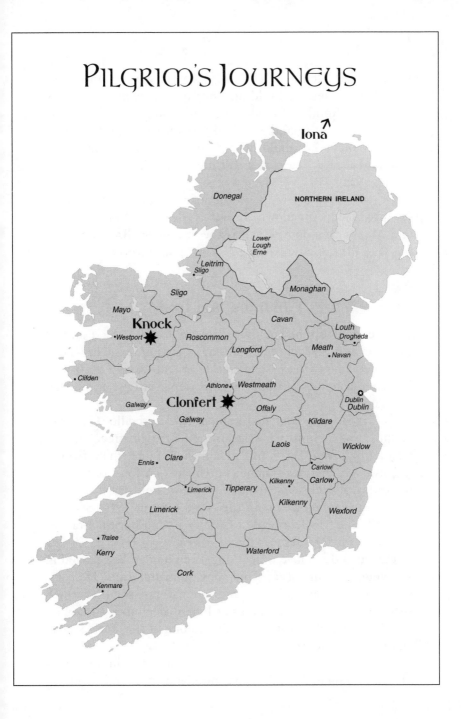

Pilgrim's Journeys

you can visit Clonfert Cathedral, a stately, extravagantly decorated Romanesque building built in the twelfth and later centuries. Brendan founded the monastery at Clonfert in County Galway around 563, and was buried here, but many people believe he would have preferred to have been laid to rest at sea, or at least on a hillside overlooking his beloved ocean.

Other sites associated with Brendan include Inishdadroum, County Clare; Annadown, County Galway; and both Ardfert and Mount Brandon (which is the site of St. Brendan's oratory and drystone monastic cells) in County Kerry.

Columba and Iona

St. Brendan left his beloved Ireland to find the Land of Promise. For St. Columba (521–597), a complex man who is esteemed among the Irish alongside St. Patrick and St. Brigid, the circumstances surrounding his departure are somewhat more controversial.

Columba, who was also known as Columcille, Colm, or Colum, was a druid who became a Christian, traveled as a wandering evangelist, and established more than twenty monasteries, the most famous of which is on Iona, one of the hundreds of Hebrides islands off the western coast of Scotland. He is revered among the Scots, and in 1910, Scottish writer Fiona Macleod called Columba "another St. Francis, because of his tenderness for creatures."

He had a deep love of learning, spending years engaged in studying, teaching others, and copying manuscripts. He composed many poems, hymns, and other works, some of which survive to this day, and it was at Iona that monks worked on the Book of Kells, which is hailed as one of the world's most amazing manuscripts.

Apparently, Columba's love of books also got him into trouble. According to legend, he borrowed a book from its well-to-do owner, but before returning it, he copied the contents of the manuscript and kept the copy for himself. The owner was unhappy about Columba's illicit copying, and went to the local king, who rendered a verdict against Columba. The head-strong Columba went to war over the issue, which resulted in the death of many of his countrymen. Fed up with Columba's impudence, the king banished him from Ireland.

We'll never know whether this legend is true, or whether Columba's exile from his beloved homeland was voluntary or imposed by others, but we do know that in 563 he and twelve fellow monks got in a boat at Derry and set sail. On Pentecost Sunday they landed on Iona, where they established one of the most important and influential Celtic monasteries.

Thanks to a biography of the saint written by a disciple named Adoman, the contemporary visitor can enjoy an informed guided tour of Iona, which is only one mile wide and three miles long, but which is overflowing with sites connected to the saint. One of the most beautiful spots is the southerly Columba's Bay, including the Port of the Coracle, which marks the spot where Columba and his disciples first came ashore. Toward the north, on the island's highest point, is Dun I, a Stone Age fort, and the Well of Eternal Youth, two of the island's many pre-Christian sites. Dominating the eastern coastal area, where most of the island's few hundred residents live, is the Abbey, which was built during the thirteenth century to house a Benedictine monastery.

This abbey is different from virtually every other site discussed in this book, for Iona's abbey isn't an abandoned ruin, but a lovingly restored church that houses a vibrant Christian community. Unlike most other Celtic sites, which were abandoned centuries ago and are now memorials to the past, Iona provides a thriving, vital link between the ancient past and the present.

The Iona Community is an ecumenical Christian group that was founded in 1938. The group seeks something they call "the rebuilding of the common life." For the community's two hundred members and its three thousand additional associates and friends, this means they try to faithfully live out the spirituality of Columba and the Christian Celts in a relevant, contemporary way.

Seven days a week, the abbey comes alive with worship services that combine reverence, spontaneity, depth, and joy. Anyone is welcome to attend these services.

In addition to worship, the community sponsors dozens of weeklong retreats and conferences, with participants staying in the abbey itself, some of the community's other buildings, or one of the nearby hotels. When the weeklong sessions aren't in progress, visitors can stay at the abbey for a minimum of three nights. In addition, you can visit the community's bookstore, coffee shop, and crafts outlet.

The community also runs a primitive-adventure camp on the nearby Isle of Mull where guests can enjoy ancient monastic touches like oil lamps (there's no electricity), peat fires (there's no furnace), and healthy exercise (all supplies have to be carried in from the nearest road, which is a mile away.)

Iona is also home to a Catholic House of Prayer where people come for retreats or periods of prayer. Father John Seddon, a priest from Liverpool, England, spent a spiritually invigorating week at the House of Prayer in 1999, and believes it is a place with its own unique mystical power. "Iona has always been one of those places that people have talked about," Father John said. "I feel like there's more to be gained from the sea around the island, or the land where the great saints have walked with God, than from the abbey or anything else."

Over the centuries, many people have visited Iona and been moved by its calming effects. Sir Walter Scott called the island "a very singular place." Felix Mendelssohn came to Iona in 1829, and the visit inspired the composition of his overture, *The Hebrides*. William Wordsworth came ashore in

1835 and wrote four separate sonnets praising the island. Today, the island still serves as a magnet for the spiritually hungry, just as it did for Columba some 1,400 years ago.

Columban's World Tour

There was a third world-wandering Irish monk, and in many ways, this man's lasting historical impact has been more significant than Brendan's or Columba's. This monk's name was Columban (c. 543–615). He was also known as Columbanus, but he is not to be confused with Columba.

Columban was a disciplined ascetic and an accomplished scholar who wrote poems and monastic Rules, but his biggest claim to fame is that he was a Celtic Billy Graham. An itinerant missionary who founded numerous Celtic-style monasteries throughout Europe, Columban helped re-Christianize the continent at a time when Germanic tribes were looting and terrorizing the formerly Christian territories of Europe. It would not be an overstatement to say that Columban did more than any other individual to spread the flame of Celtic Christianity throughout the world. Celtic scholar Gerhard Herm described Columban's journeys as "one of the great missionary feats of the church's history." Or as Sean McMahon put it: "He remains the great Irishman of Europe who relit the light that was not to be quenched." Today, one can still find his imprint all over Europe.

Columban and his band of twelve Celtic monks left Ireland in 591 for France, where they established numerous monastic outposts, the most famous of which was Luxeil, located about 230 miles southeast of Paris at the modern-day city of Luxeil-les-Bains. Soon, Irish monasteries were appearing all across the French countryside, including centers at Laon, Angoulême on the Charente River in the west, Peronne on the Somme River in the north, and Liège in what is now French-speaking Belgium.

The Celtic tradition of pilgrimage is alive at Knock in County Mayo.
Every year more than a million people visit the site where the Virgin
Mary appeared to townspeople in 1879.

They went to Germany, establishing centers at Aachen in
the Westphalia region, and Wurzburg in Bavaria—a site that
remains a popular destination for Irish pilgrims. They went to
Austria, founding a monastery at an old pagan temple site at
Bregenz, a town near Lake Constance near the border
between Germany and Switzerland. In Switzerland, they set
up a center at Reichenau, located on an island in Lake Constance. St. Gall, one of Columban's original twelve disciples,
elected not to cross the Alps with his hard-charging leader,
and instead remained behind and created the important
center of St. Gallen (or Sankt Gallen), located forty-five miles
east of Zurich. They went to Italy, founding Bobbio, a

monastery fifty miles south of Milan, which was still going strong when St. Francis visited it in the early 1200s, and might still be in business today were it not for the fact that Napoleon shut it down in the early nineteenth century. The Irish monks also established a center at Lucca, way down in Tuscany, along with centers at Auxerre, Fiesole, Fulda, Lumieges, Regensburg, Rhienau, Trier, Salzburg, and Vienna.

Like some latter-day Apostle Paul, Columban was reportedly rescued from drowning, freed from prison, and given power over wild wolves and bears. Thanks to his tireless efforts and his unquenchable wanderlust, the spirit of Celtic Christianity was spread throughout much of the known world.

Knocking on Heaven's Door

Today, the Celtic spirit of pilgrimage is alive at Knock, which until August 21, 1879, was a peaceful little village in County Mayo. On that day, the Virgin Mary allegedly appeared to more than a dozen townspeople, her image superimposed on the side of the parish church. Knock has been a pilgrimage site ever since, and along with Lourdes in France and Fatima in Portugal, has become one of Europe's foremost Marian shrines. Its popularity grew in 1979 when Pope John Paul II held a Mass there for 450,000 people in honor of the shrine's centenary. Now, with 1.5 million visitors every year, many of them traveling on charter flights into the specially built Knock International Airport, Knock is Ireland's busiest tourist destination.

Over the years, Knock has grown and evolved. The simple little church where Mary first appeared is now surrounded by a complex of buildings and plazas, including a 10,000-seat Basilica, a Blessed Sacrament Chapel, a Chapel of Reconciliation, a pilgrim's Prayer Center, and at the center of it all, the Apparition Chapel. Alongside Processional Square, which is one of the complex's central plazas, are eighteen modern-looking, push-button holy-water fonts made out of carved marble. Nearby are a religious bookstore, a hostel, a folk museum, souvenir shops, and a post office, and farther away are parking areas for cars, buses, and campers.

For many, Knock is the modern equivalent of an ancient holy shrine, and the crowds that assemble there on important feast days and celebrations are seen as the latest incarnation of a Celtic tradition that's been going on for millenia. But others aren't so sure.

Liam Fay is an Irish rock journalist and religious satirist who visited Knock and declared it to be "a bizarre and distasteful place." Fay was disgusted by the commercialism of the place, which he said was full of "Knock knickknacks," as well as an overall air of showmanship, which he disdainfully described:

> Its stock in trade is a treacly, catchpenny concoction of superstition and tinsel, trumpery and schmaltz, all served up in gluttonous heapfuls and doled out like manure off a shiny shovel.

Clearly, Knock isn't for everybody, but for millions of people this shrine is a sacred place where the ancient Celtic belief in the immanence of God is finding a compelling contemporary expression.

Joy in the Journey

There is much today's traveler can learn from yesterday's Celtic pilgrims, whose zeal for wandering was summarized nicely by scholar Lisa Bitel in her book *Isle of the Saints:*

> ... the most profound expression of monastic spirituality was to sever all social ties and march out of the gates of the sacred enclosure into the wilderness, never looking back. Irishmen became famous for the self-imposed exiles and pilgrimages that took them far from the security of home. The greatest heroes of Irish monasticism were vagrants. . . .

Celts like these transformed the near-universal metaphor of life as a journey into a living reality, boldly venturing out into the world with a powerful combination of passion, wide-eyed wonder, and faith.

Some modern travelers may not want to mimic the Celts' navigational techniques. In *The Voyage of Maeldune*, a saintly legend with many similarities to Brendan's *Navigatio*, Maeldune tells his lost and lonely men, "Leave the boat quiet without rowing, and wherever God has a mind to bring it, let it go." While some might consider such tales mere fantasy, the *Anglo-Saxon Chronicle*, one of a number of early British histories, reports that at least one group of pilgrims followed Maeldune's advice. The chronicle reports that in 891 three Celtic monks:

> . . . came to King Alfred in a boat without oars from Ireland whence they stole away, because they would be in a state of pilgrimage for the love of God, they recked not where.

One might be tempted to call these monks aimless, but in reality, their aim was clear: to make themselves available to go wherever God would send them. One may quibble with their technique, but we can think of far worse approaches to travel—an activity that can transform us if we let it.

PART II

Getting There

10

Tips for the Journey

General Information
for Planning Your Trip

The following pages contain a wealth of practical information designed to make your journey to Ireland more successful and more rewarding. All information listed here is correct at press time, but please check information on your own before booking a trip.

Note: We use the term *Ireland* to refer to the entire island, both north and south. When relevant, we will use "Republic of Ireland" when referring to the independent southern nation, and "Northern Ireland" when referring to the British province.

Air Travel

The Republic of Ireland has three international airports, but unless you're traveling on a charter flight to the pilgrimage site at Knock, you will be flying into Dublin in the east or Shannon in the west. Both are serviced by major carriers from several United States cities. When calling the airline simply tell them your hometown airport, and they will give you fares and schedules to connect with direct overseas flights.

Aer Lingus is the Republic of Ireland's major air carrier with regular service from New York, Newark, Boston, Chicago, and Los Angeles to Dublin and/or Shannon. Continental Airlines offers direct service from Newark Airport to Dublin and Shannon, and Delta Airlines flies directly from Atlanta to Dublin and Shannon. Connections may also be made through London to Dublin and Shannon.

Northern Ireland is serviced by Belfast International Airport with hourly flights on British Airways or British Midland from Heathrow International Airport in London.

Travel tip: if you are making connections in Heathrow, allow plenty of time—at least two hours—as this is one of the busiest airports in the world.

Airlines that fly from the United States to Ireland:

Aer Lingus	800-IRISH AIR
Aeroflot	888-340-6400
American Trans Air	800-435-9282
Continental Airlines	800-231-0856
Delta Airlines	800-241-4141

Major airlines that fly from the United States and Canada to cities in Britain (connections through London to Ireland and Northern Ireland):

Air Canada	800-776-3000;
	800-268-7240 (in Canada)
Air India	800-223-7776;
	212-751-6200 (in New York City)
American Airlines	800-433-7300
British Airways	800-247-9297
Continental Airlines	800-231-0856

Delta Airlines	800-241-4141
Northwest Airlines	800-447-4747
United Airlines	800-241-6522
Virgin Atlantic	800-862-8621

Booking Air Travel Online

While many online offers appear to be the best deals possible, be careful. Read all regulations and agreements before committing to purchasing a ticket. For instance, when submitting a request for information on some online services, you are actually committing to a ticket *purchase* that may not be canceled.

Bestfares.Com Editor Tom Parsons advises, "The Internet gives you a place to do research, but don't take everything as gospel. Don't think it's the cheapest price—even if it says so."

Baggage Restrictions

Airline regulations for carry-on baggage have changed in the last few years and airline crews strictly enforce these rules. When booking reservations, ask for information about current checked and carry-on luggage requirements. Some airlines allow fewer carry-on bags for international travel than they do for domestic travel.

Travel Agents

While some travel agents now charge for services, most do not charge for making international arrangements. Sometimes even a small fee might be worth the cost to avail yourself of the experience of professionals.

Car Rental

Make car rental reservations before leaving North America. The rate will be cheaper and you'll avoid the hassle of booking while in Ireland. Be sure to tell the car agency if you will be taking the car across the border between the Republic of Ireland and Northern Ireland, and check to make sure the insurance will cover you in both countries.

Also check with your credit card company to see if they cover foreign car rental insurance in their benefit package. It's best to call the credit card company as some offer international coverage but exclude Ireland. American Express and Visa are two companies who have this policy.

Travel tip: Ask for rates on cars with standard transmissions, as they are generally a lot less expensive than cars with automatic transmissions.

Major car rental agencies:

Alamo	800-522-9696
Avis	800-331-1084
Budget	800-472-3325
Dan Dooley	800-331-9301
Hertz	800-654-3001

Driving in Ireland

Start slowly. You will be driving on the left-hand side of the road and often on very narrow, winding thoroughfares, unfamiliar to most American drivers. And as soon as you leave the airport you will be faced with your first roundabout, which is the Emerald Isle's answer to the intersection. You will be pulling into moving traffic going around in a circle and exiting at various roads spoking out from the circle. This may sound daunting, but once you get the hang of it you'll wonder why we use so many traffic lights.

Distances in Northern Ireland are measured in miles, while all new road signs in the Republic of Ireland are measured in kilometers. Older signs in the Republic may still be in miles. In both countries, gasoline is sold in liters. Remember, 1 mile equals 1.6 kilometers; and 1 gallon equals 3.8 liters.

A good map is imperative. Three major designations tell you the kind of road to expect: M—divided highways or motorways; N—two lanes with shoulders on which to pass; and R—two-lane, narrow, regional roads.

Route numbers are often not printed on road signs, so look ahead on your map for the name of towns along the way. Then follow the directional signs for the next town on your route.

Travel tip: purchase a Michelin Motoring Atlas of Great Britain and Ireland before leaving home. Most major bookstores carry them and the cost will be well worth it. The navigator helping the driver with directions should keep this road bible close at hand every moving minute.

When crossing from the Republic of Ireland to Northern Ireland, you may encounter some border checkpoints. These generally pose no problem for tourists and cause little inconvenience. Have your passport handy in case you are asked for it.

You will often be driving in rural areas where sheep graze along road shoulders and wander into traffic. The sheep have the right of way, so be patient.

Patience is the key to enjoyable driving in this rugged land. Don't aim to cover lots of miles but allow time to reduce speed and increase pleasure.

Train and Bus Travel

In the Republic of Ireland rail service is available between all principal towns and Dublin. Train travel between smaller villages is not direct and can be time-consuming. In Northern Ireland there are three main routes operating out of Belfast: north to Derry, east to Bangor, and south to Dublin.

Bus service links most cities with scheduled service.
For information and reservations, call Irish Rail and Irish
Bus at 800-243-7687.

Travel tip: If visiting Celtic sites is one of your primary goals,
it is easiest and most convenient to travel by car.

Customs and Duties

United States residents may bring back $400 per person worth
of duty-free merchandise. You may also ship packages to your
home. The limit on these purchases is $200. But some manu-
facturers, like Waterford crystal and Belleek china, pay the
duty for you. It is best to ask the seller when making purchases above your allowance what the specific policy is.

Keep all receipts and be ready to show customs officials
what you've purchased.

For specific questions about exceptions or taxable amounts
over the duty-free allowance, call U. S. Customs Service in
Washington, D. C. at 202-354-1000; www.customs.gov.

Valued-Added Tax (VAT)

A 12.5 to 21 percent refund is given to U.S. residents at many
of the shops and stores throughout the Republic of Ireland
and Northern Ireland. These goods often list two sale prices:
retail and export. The export price is the amount you will
have paid after you receive your refund. Some refunds are
given at the time of purchase and others are credited to you
after you return home.

Procedures for claiming your refund vary with the store, so
just ask each time you make a purchase if there is a VAT due.
This is a very routine practice and you will find salespeople
happy to give you the proper advice.

Passports and Visas

U. S. citizens traveling to Ireland and Northern Ireland need a valid passport. No visa is necessary. For passport applications, call your local passport office listed in the U. S. Government pages of your telephone book.

Once you have obtained your passport, make several copies of the data page. Leave one copy at home with a friend or relative and pack one separately from your passport. In case of loss while you are away, go to the U. S. embassy or consulate. You will need the copy of your data page or other proof of citizenship such as a birth certificate.

Travel tip: Ireland is one of the safest countries in which to travel. However, you can't be too careful with your passport.

Electricity

The electrical current in Ireland is 220 volts (AC). If you take North American electrical equipment you will need a converter and adapter. Most laptop computers require only an adapter.

Money

The currency in the Republic of Ireland is the Irish pound or punt. While the money has the word *punt* printed on it, most people speak in terms of pounds.

In Northern Ireland the currency is the pound sterling, the same currency as Great Britain. Money between the two countries is not interchangeable.

Before leaving the United States you can check the rate of exchange in the business section of most major newspapers. As of January 31, 2001, the punt stood at around U.S. $1.17. So, if an item cost 20 punt, it would be the equivalent of

$23.40; multiply the punt amount by the dollar equivalent, or 20 × 1.17 = $23.40.

The best way to carry money overseas is in the form of traveler's checks. If you are a member of the American Automobile Association there is no fee for obtaining traveler's checks. You might also check with your local bank and see what fee they charge. Call a few weeks before your departure in case they need to order checks for you.

When exchanging dollars (or traveler's checks) for Irish pounds, the best rate of exchange will usually be at a bank. Other agencies, like tourist offices and hotels, are often able to exchange money for you but the fee may be more than at a bank.

International airports will also have money exchange windows for your convenience upon arrival.

Travel tip: Just as money is different between the Republic of Ireland and Northern Ireland, so are postal rates and stamps—be sure to use stamps from the country where you are mailing cards or letters or your messages may never arrive.

Telephones

For emergency calls for police, fire, medical, dial 999.

Making phone calls in a foreign country can be exasperating, even when there is no language barrier. So don't panic when you first try to make a call.

When making calls within the country there are public phones that take coins and ones that take phone cards. If you anticipate needing to make calls within the Republic of Ireland or Northern Ireland, it's easier to purchase a phone card than to keep a ready supply of coins. These cards can be purchased at the airport upon arrival in various denominations ranging from 10 to 100 units. A unit is worth 20 pence or about $.32.

In making long-distance calls back to the United States you will need the access code for the long distance service you use. If your long distance provider is not listed below, call the company before leaving home and find out the procedure for calling from overseas.

Access Codes: after dialing the appropriate access code, follow the prompts and have your phone credit card available.

AT&T: calling from the Republic of Ireland 1-800-550000
AT&T: calling from Northern Ireland 0-800-0130011
MCI: calling from the Republic of Ireland 1-800-5551001
MCI: calling from Northern Ireland
   0-800-890222 using BT
   0-500-890222 using Mercury
Sprint Express: calling from the Republic of Ireland
   1-800-552001
Sprint Express: calling from Northern Ireland
   0-800-890877 using BT
   0-500-890877 using Mercury

If you need additional assistance, call the international operator:

In Ireland: 114
In Northern Ireland: 155

When calling from the United States to Ireland dial 011 + country code + city code + number. The country code for the Republic of Ireland is 353; Northern Ireland is 44. City and country codes are listed with phone numbers in the A to Z Guide in this book.

Travel tip: Make a copy of your phone company's access code and carry it with you. Most of your calls will be made from public phones, as many bed and breakfasts don't have phones with long distance capabilities for their guests.

Packing

You've heard it before: Pack light! Unless you have a special event to attend or are staying in expensive hotels, you won't need dressy clothes. However, even in summer you need room to pack a heavy sweater and waterproof jacket or coat and an umbrella. Slacks, washable shirts, polos or blouses, and comfortable shoes are the norm for day or evening.

Most hotels and B&Bs have hair dryers available. If there isn't one in your room, ask the proprietor if you may borrow one. This is the time for ladies to sport their most simple hairstyle and eliminate the need for curling irons and other hair supplies.

If you are staying in B&Bs, take along a bar of soap from home. Many supply soap, but not all do. Another useful item is a travel clothesline with clothespins. These compact items can be useful when washing out underwear and socks. This way you can save space by bringing only a few pairs and hand laundering them. Many towns have drop-off laundries where you can leave larger clothing items in the morning and pick them up in the afternoon. The cost is reasonable and the service is very convenient.

Travel tip: Order quick-dry travel underwear from the Travel-Smith catalog. These are available for men and women and are comfortable, dry overnight items. We traveled for four weeks with a few pair each and loved them. Call 1-800-950-1600.

Make sure to bring any medication you'll need, an extra pair of glasses, a travel journal, and a travel alarm. You may only need the alarm on days when you need to catch a ferry, but then it'll really come in handy.

If you are a postcard writer, print address labels before leaving home for the postcards you'll be sending. Then as you travel you will have a built-in list of people you want to send cards to, you'll save time addressing cards, and your cards will most likely arrive sooner.

It's also a good idea to pack an extra bag to bring home goodies that you purchase along the way. Choose a foldable material like vinyl that you can fold up and pack in your other luggage.

Shopping

Many wonderful delights await the traveling shopper. Among the best values are Aran sweaters, Irish crystal, Irish ceramics, woolens, Irish linen, traditional jewelry, and Irish whiskey. Duty-free shops also have good values on items that are manufactured in other European countries. Those include perfumes, watches, silks, and leather goods.

If you have a particular item you are hoping to purchase at a savings, do some research before leaving home. Price your favorite perfume, Waterford crystal, Wedgwood china, or woolen suit. Compare prices when you arrive and see if you are really saving.

Travel tip: Take a written list of prices with you, because savings vary dramatically depending on the item. For example, when pricing perfume in a duty-free shop at the airport I found that Chanel No. 5 had much greater reductions than Shalimar. If I had not had a written list with me from home, I could never have remembered the prices in order to compare.

Heritage Cards

Many of the Republic of Ireland's visitor attractions are part of the Heritage Service. With the purchase of a Heritage Card you may visit any of these sites free of charge. (See the A–Z Guide in this book for the Heritage sites.) The cost is approximately $20.00 per adult. The cards are available at any site location along with a list of all other Heritage Sites including parks, monuments, gardens, and inland waterways.

Time

Ireland is on the same time as Great Britain. It is five hours ahead of East Coast time, six hours ahead of Central time, seven hours ahead of Mountain time and eight hours ahead of Pacific time.

Lodging

A wide range of accommodations are available throughout Ireland and Northern Ireland, from elegant hotels, castles, and estates to charming bed and breakfasts.

In the A–Z Guide in this book, each major city or town listing will include several options with a recommendation from us of some places we especially enjoyed. Most of the time we opted for B&Bs, staying at hotels only in larger cities.

Rates quoted generally include a full Irish breakfast.

You can make reservations when you arrive in Ireland, but during the most popular travel times (June through September) it is often good to book in advance. At the end of this section references are listed for more complete lodging options.

Travel tip: Keep the time difference in mind if you are calling from the United States to make advance reservations. You might wake up a proprietor or waste a call by getting an answering machine.

Dining

Almost every day begins with the opportunity to indulge in a full Irish breakfast, which consists of eggs, bacon, sausage, black pudding, grilled tomato, bread, fruit, cereal, juice, and coffee or tea. Don't worry, you can allay your health concerns since traveling around Ireland usually involves a lot of walking.

Other specialities include lamb, fish, and wonderful vegetable dishes, especially potatoes. Of course, afternoon tea is accompanied by delicious scones or pastries.

Menus in restaurants, cafes, tea rooms, and pubs offer a variety of dishes in many price ranges. Pub menus have expanded in recent years, making these traditional establishments a fine choice for budget dining. Tea rooms are often attached to an attraction or site and are set up like North American cafeterias. They are pleasant, convenient when sightseeing, and economical.

Keep in mind that restaurants don't usually begin to serve dinner until 7:00 P.M., and you may need reservations. Your hotel concierge or B&B host will be glad to book a table for you.

Web Sites

The following sites can help you with your trip planning:

www.paddynet.com (Irish sites)
www.ireland.travel.ie (Irish Tourism Board)
www.ni-tourism.com (Northern Ireland Tourist Board)
www.commerce.ie/towns_and_country/ (B&B lodgings)

Helpful Reference Material

The following tourist boards and travel books will also provide you with additional information about all aspects of travel in Ireland:

Irish Tourist Board (New York): 800-223-6470; offers many publications that list B&Bs, attractions, and general information.

Northern Ireland Tourist Board (New York): 800-326-0036; offers many publications that list B&Bs, attractions, and general information.

Fodor's Ireland: A comprehensive travel guide, updated yearly (Web site: http://fodors.previewtravel.com).

DK Eyewitness Travel Guides: *Ireland* (includes Northern Ireland); Web site: www.dk.com.

Dublin Tourist Center: See Dublin in the A–Z Guide in this book.

Regional Tourist Offices: See major cities in the A–Z Guide in this book.

11

Λ-Ζ Guide

SITES, CITIES, AND MAJOR
POINTS OF INTEREST

As you begin the adventure of planning your journey through Ireland, this section can help you. Whether you're creating your own itinerary or following one of the itineraries we've suggested in the next chapter, this guide will help you get to and from the major sites described in the book.

Listings for major cities include suggestions for lodging and dining and give you the essentials for enjoying the cities themselves. Since a number of sites are near smaller towns, these towns will be listed to help you determine day stops while touring.

The site listings will give you details about location, opening and closing times, and cost. Costs are denoted by £ for Republic of Ireland pounds and by U.K.£ for Northern Ireland pounds sterling.

Other points of interest are not necessarily Celtic sites but are areas or places you may find interesting as you travel.

Note: All the information presented here is correct at press time, but please check all prices and times on your own before

155

visiting a site, particularly if you are making a detour to see
something.

Aran Islands, Co. Galway

These three rocky Atlantic islands are rich in pagan and Christian ruins. Most of the following information pertains to Inishmore, the largest of the Aran Islands, which is most important
and easiest to get to. Travel information to Inishmaan and
Inisheer is included under "Travel to the Aran Islands" below.

Sites

Dun Aengus is one of the most impressive Iron Age forts in
the world. In addition, numerous early Christian ruins are
found throughout Inishmore, including the site of St. Enda's
monastery at the island's western end; the Seven Churches, a
monastic settlement dedicated to St. Brecan, that lies at the
far eastern end of the island; and a holy well.

• **Dun Aengus Fort,** southwestern side of Inishmore, four
miles west of the boat dock.

Massive, majestic, and set on an an amazing clifftop location, admission to this ancient fort is free and is open to the
public all the time.

Travel to the Aran Islands

The Aran Islands lie in the Atlantic Ocean some thirty miles
west of the mouth of Galway Bay.

AIR TRAVEL   Aer Arann operates daily flights to Inishmore,
Inishmaan, and Inisheer all year round. Flights leave from the
Connemara Regional Airport, Inverin, Co. Galway, twenty-
eight miles east of Galway. During the summer season flights
operate approximately every hour. Flight time is approximately ten minutes. There is bus service from Galway and

Salthill (suburb of Galway) to meet every flight. Fares: adult round trip £35.00, children round trip £20.00. Telephone: 353-91-593-034; fax: 353-91-593-238; e-mail: aer arann@iol.it.

FERRY TRAVEL Two ferry companies operate to the Aran Islands.

Island Ferries has service from Rosaveel to all three islands. Bus service is available from Galway to Rosaveel or it is an easy thirty-three-mile drive along the coast. Reservations can be made before leaving the United States which assures you of passage during high season. Travel time between Rosaveel and the Aran Islands is thirty minutes. Schedule for Inishmore: April 1–October 31, daily leave Rosaveel for Inishmore 10:30 A.M., 1:30 P.M., 6:30 P.M.; daily leave Inishmore for Rosaveel 9:00 A.M., 12:00 P.M., 5:00 P.M., and 7:30 P.M. Additional sailings added during July and August. November–March, daily leave Rosaveel for Inishmore 10:30 A.M., 5:30 P.M.; daily leave Inishmore for Rosaveel 9:00 A.M., 4:00 P.M. Schedule for Inishmaan and Inisheer: May–September, daily leave Rosaveel 10:30 A.M.; daily leave islands 4:00 P.M. Fares: adult, £15.00. Telephone: 353-91-561-767; fax: 353-91-568-538. Inter Island Service: 353-91-566-398.

O'Brien Shipping has service from Galway to all three islands. Travel time is ninety minutes. Schedule: June–September, daily leave Galway 10:30 A.M.; daily leave Inishmore 5:00 P.M.; October–May, Tuesday, Thursday, Saturday, leave Galway 10:30 A.M.; leave Inishmore 5:00 P.M. Fare: approximately £18.00 for adults round trip. Telephone: 353-91-567-283. Fax: 353-91-567-672.

Arriving in the Aran Islands

The dock at Inishmore is a bustling place with minivans and jaunting cars (pony-drawn two-wheel carts) lined up to take you all over the island. Resist the overly aggressive drivers and wander on toward Kilronan, the center of your land-

ing village. It is a very short walk and you will have the opportunity to compare prices or decide if you would like to tour by
bicycle. The price for minivans and carts may be cheaper if
you walk away from the dock and don't look overly eager.
Some of the vans leaving from the village instead of the pier
charge £5.00 per person as opposed to the £10.00 at the pier.
Bicycle rental is £5.00 for the day. Advance booking for bicycles is not necessary but you can do so with Aran Bicycle Hire.
Telephone: 353-99-61132.

Lodging

Many travelers stay in Galway and visit the Aran Islands for
the day. If you decide to give these lovely islands more than a
passing glance, Inishmore does have several B&Bs. We've
listed a few, our favorite being the Kilmurvey House.

- **An Crugan,** Inishmore, Aran Islands. This B&B is only a
  ten-minute walk from the pier, close to restaurants, pubs,
  and shops. There are six rooms, five ensuite, at a rate of
  approximately £25.00 per person per night. Telephone: 353-
  99-61468.

- **Cregmount House,** Inishmore, Aran Islands. Beautiful
  views from an unspoiled location. There are three rooms,
  one ensuite. Rates are approximately £25.00 per person per
  night. Telephone: 353-99-61139.

- **Kilmurvey House,** Inishmore, Aran Islands. We didn't stay
  overnight but had a lovely visit with owner Treasa Joyce.
  This beautiful eighteenth-century stone farmhouse has history and ambience. A number of well-known Americans
  stay here when wanting to enjoy peace, quiet, and the
  absence of the media. The house is located right next to
  Dun Aengus Fort with a small cluster of shops and a wonderful little restaurant, the Teac Nan Paidi, a stone's throw
  away. Irish breakfast is included in the price and dinner is

available every evening for an additional £14.00 per person. All twelve rooms are ensuite. MasterCard and Visa are accepted. Rates are £20.00 per person per night in April, May, June, September and October; £25.00 per person in July and August. Closed November–March. Telephone: 353-99-61218; fax: 353-99-61397.

Dining

- **Teac Nan Paidi,** Inishmore, next to Dun Aengus Fort. Wonderful afternoon meals at reasonable prices. Great lunch stop when touring the fort.

- **The Dun Aonghasa Seafood Restaurant and Bar,** Inishmore. Overlooking Kileaney Bay, the Dun Aonghasa serves creative island dishes based on the tradition of the Arans. They also offer fresh seafood. Telephone: 353-99-61104; fax: 353-99-61225.

- **The Aran Fisherman,** Kilronan Village, Inishmore. This casual restaurant is conveniently located in the village near the pier. A good stop for tea before heading off on a long bike ride or for refreshments after a day of touring. Snacks and meals served all day.

Shopping

About a dozen small shops are conveniently located a short walk from the pier. Another group of shops are right next to the road leading up to Dun Aengus Fort. Of course, the speciality of the islands are the Aran sweaters, traditional woolen sweaters knitted by local people. Prices are comparable to those on the mainland and a purchase here may add to the authenticity of your travel memories. The designs of these sweaters indicate different families and were worn by fishermen to fight the cold of the windy Atlantic Ocean. If the worst occurred and fishing boats went down, the men could be identified by the pattern of their sweaters.

Services and Amenities

In Kilronan village there is a grocery store, pay phones accepting credit cards, and the Aran Heritage Center. The Heritage Center regularly shows the movie *The Man of Aran*, filmed on the island in 1934. There is also an interpretive display, audiovisual presentation, and gift shop. Open: April–October, daily 10:00 A.M.–7:00 P.M. Telephone: 353-99-61355.

Armagh, Co. Armagh, N. Ireland

Once an important pagan center, Armagh was where St. Patrick founded his diocese.

Sites

- **Navan Fort** was once one of Ireland's most legendary pagan sites, though there isn't much to see now. Located two and a half miles west of Armagh, the fort is free of charge and is always open to the public.

- **Navan Centre,** adjacent to Navan Fort. This center interprets the archaeology and mythology of the site. It includes a film and interactive displays. Open: April–June, and September, Monday–Friday 10:00 A.M.–6:00 P.M., Saturday 11:00 A.M.–6:00 P.M., Sunday 12:00–6:00 P.M.; July–August, Monday–Saturday 10:00 A.M.–7:00 P.M., Sunday 11:00 A.M.–7:00 P.M.; October–March, Monday–Friday 10:00 A.M.–5:00 P.M., Saturday 11:00 A.M.–5:00 P.M., Sunday 12:00–5:00 P.M. Admission: U.K.£3.95. Telephone: 44-28-3752-5550.

- **St. Patrick's Catholic Cathedral and St. Patrick's Protestant Cathedral.** The Protestant church, which is older, used to be a Catholic church. The newer Catholic church, with its mosaic floors and lofty ceiling, is much more impressive. Both are generally open for visitors.

Location

Armagh is forty miles west of Belfast and 48 miles east of Enniskillen.

Lodging

- **Drumsill Hotel,** one mile northwest of Armagh. This modern hotel is located on fifteen acres of wooded grounds and offers clean and functional rooms. The Gallery Restaurant serves a creative menu, and Bond's Wine Bar features live music on weekends. Ten rooms all ensuite. Rates range from U.K.£70.00–U.K.£135.00 per room per night. Telephone: 44-28-3752-2009; fax: 44-28-3752-5624.

Dining

There are a number of restaurants in Armagh with a wide range of choices and prices.

Athlone, Co. Westmeath

If your visit to Clonmacnois (see listing) doesn't allow for a drive to Galway or Dublin, you can spend the night in Athlone. A few B&Bs are located in this small river town. You can take a boat from the dock across from the Athlone Castle to Clonmacnois if time allows.

Belfast, Co. Antrim, N. Ireland

This storied town is an excellent jumping-off point for trips to Downpatrick, Grey Abbey, and the Nendrum monastic island site.

Location

Belfast is located 104 miles north of Dublin.

Lodging

Belfast has a number of B&Bs and large hotels. We have listed our favorite of each.

- **Ash-Rowan Townhouse,** 12 Windsor Ave. Located on a peaceful, tree-lined street in the university area, time spent here makes one forget that Belfast ever suffered from the Troubles. Sam and Evelyn Hazlett are gracious hosts who have adorned this Victorian property, once the home of *Titanic* designer Thomas Andrews, with antique furnishings and accessories. Each of the eight bedrooms has direct dial phone, TV, and all are ensuite. Rates are U.K.£40.00 to U.K.£70.00. Telephone: 44-28-9066-1758; fax: 44-28-9066-2227.

- **The McCausland Hotel,** 34-38 Victoria Street. This luxury hotel, while in the expensive category, is a five-minute walk to the city center and provides all the conveniences for a restful stay in a busy city. It is sparkling clean with a décor of modern, clean lines. There are sixty rooms with bath. Rates are over U.K.£135.00 per night. Telephone: 44-28-9022-0200; fax: 44-28-9022-0220.

Dining

Belfast has numerous fine restaurants. Check with your B&B or hotel host for suggestions.

Services and Amenities

Belfast is a full-service city.

Blarney Castle, Blarney, Co. Cork

Blarney Castle, six miles northwest of Cork, draws crowds of visitors from all over the world who are seeking the gift of eloquent and witty speech by kissing the Blarney Stone. Getting to the stone and positioning yourself for the famous kiss may be a bit of a challenge; after descending 127 steps, you have to lie on your back, hold on to a guardrail, and stretch way back. It is a safe caper but there's no guarantee as to your personal verbal results.

The castle itself is a ruin with the central keep being all that remains.

If you do decide to go for the kiss, you may want to stop in the town of Blarney and visit some of the many craft shops and the Blarney Woolen Mills (telephone: 353-21-385-280). The Mills are well known throughout Ireland and sell quality Irish goods at competitive prices.

Book of Kells, Trinity College, Dublin

See listing for Dublin.

Browneshill Dolmen, Co. Carlow

Lying in the middle of an easy-to-miss field two miles east of the town of Carlow stands the Browneshill Dolmen, reputed to have the largest capstone of any megalithic tomb in Europe. The location is poorly marked, so be prepared to ask directions from local folks. This site is free and accessible all the time.

Cahirsiveen, Co. Kerry

Cahirsiveen is the main market town and shopping center for South Kerry, but we are listing it because it is the prime jumping-off spot for a trip out into the Atlantic Ocean and the island of Skellig Michael.

Sites

- **Skellig Heritage Centre,** Valentia Island, Ring of Kerry. Valentia Island is just off the coast by Cahirsiveen and can be reached by road or a very short car and ferry ride. The center features an exhibition of the history of the Skellig islands, including displays that highlight the monks who inhabited rocky Skellig Michael for centuries, and the more recent history of the Skellig Lighthouse. An excellent sixteen-minute audiovisual show takes visitors out to the monastic ruins for a look through the camera lens at this amazing site. The center also has a gift shop and lovely little tea room with views looking out over the harbor toward the Skelligs. Open April–September daily.

- **Skellig Michael Monastery.** See listing for Skellig Michael Monastery.

Location

Cahirsiveen is eleven miles northwest of Waterville on the Ring of Kerry road.

Lodging

There are a number of B&Bs scattered along the coastal road in and around Cahirsiveen. Many of these afford breathtaking views of the Atlantic Ocean, with glimpses of the Skellig Islands.

Dining

Cahirsiveen has a number of pubs and small restaurants, and we've listed two that we especially enjoyed.

- **Brennan's Restaurant.** Right in the middle of town on the main street, this small but stylish restaurant offers a varied and delicious menu. It is a very nice spot for a lovely evening meal. Prices are from £20.00 to £25.00 per person for a full meal.

- **O'Neill's the Point,** Renard Point. This casual seafood bar and restaurant overlooks Valentia Harbor and offers an absolutely delicious menu. The seafood is fresh and the proprietors, Michael and Brigid O'Neill, are personable and welcoming. Prices range from £8.00 to £12.00 per person. Telephone: 353-66-94-72165; fax: 353-66-94-72068.

Services and Amenities

While Cahirsiveen is small it does offer most services that any traveler would need. There are a number of gas stations, grocery stores, banks, a post office, and a drop-off laundry.

Carlow, Co. Carlow

Carlow, twenty-three miles northeast of Kilkenny, is a delightfully typical Irish town peppered with pubs and friendly people. It's a good lunch stop while exploring the surrounding area.

Teach Dolmain, one of the local pubs that serves good bar food, portrays the dolmen period of Carlow in its decor and pottery. Meals are reasonably priced and range from soups and scones to sandwiches and main courses.

Carrowkeel, Co. Sligo

See listing under Sligo.

Carrowmore, Co. Sligo

This megalithic cemetery rests in the lush, rolling countryside about eight miles south of Sligo. Guided tours are available and colorfully inform visitors about the site itself as well as the surrounding historic landscape. A small exhibition center housed in an old cottage is the beginning point. Open May–September, daily 9:30 A.M.–6:30 P.M. Admission: free with Heritage Card; adults £1.50, children £0.60. Senior and group discounts available. Telephone: 353-71-61534.

Cashel, Co. Tipperary

Victorian storefronts grace the main street of the market town of Cashel. Located twelve miles northeast of Tipperary Town, Cashel is most known for one of Ireland's most famous sites (see the Rock of Cashel).

Visitors will find other points of interest after visiting the Rock, including:

- **The Bru Boru Heritage Center,** at the base of the Rock of Cashel. The Center features exhibits on many aspects of Irish life and offers folk theater, traditional music, banquets, a craft shop, a genealogy center, and a restaurant. Open June–October, daily 9:00 A.M.–6 P.M.; November–May, daily 9:00 A.M.– 5:00 P.M. Admission: free with Heritage Card; evening song and storytelling £5.00. Telephone: 353-62-61122.

Clonmacnois, Co. Offaly

Once one of Ireland's most important monastic complexes, the site now has an impressive number of remains.

Clonmacnois is located four miles north of Shannonbrige and thirteen miles south of Athlone. Open November–mid March, daily 10:00 A.M.–5:30 P.M.; mid March–mid May, daily 10:00 A.M.–6:00 P.M.; mid May–early September, daily 9:00 A.M.–7:00 P.M.; September–October, daily 10:00 A.M.–6:00 P.M. Admission: free with Heritage Card; adults £3.00, children £1.25. Senior citizen, family, and group discounts available.

Telephone: 353-905-74195; fax: 353-905-74273. This is a very busy site and visitors may experience a wait during the summer months.

Creevykeel, Co. Sligo

See listing under Sligo.

Croagh Patrick, Co. Mayo

Long an important pilgrimage sight and allegedly the place where St. Patrick fasted and prayed for forty days, this brooding, conical mountain overlooks Clew Bay and is located five miles west of the town of Westport. Croagh Patrick is free and open all the time.

Dingle, Co. Kerry

This charming coastal town is on the beautiful Dingle peninsula, which is rich in history and archaeology.

Sites

- **Dunbeg Fort.** About ten miles west of Dingle town, the fort is one of the best-preserved examples of an Iron Age promontory fort. There is a small entrance fee.

- **Gallarus Oratory.** This Christian building is an excellent example of Irish drystone construction, and is located about six miles northwest of Dingle town.

Location

Dingle is located on the Dingle Peninsula, forty-two miles west of Killarney.

Lodging and Dining

There are a number of B&Bs and a few small hotels. We had a very pleasant evening including an outstanding meal in one of them and share it with you in the listing below.

- **Doyle's Seafood Bar and Town House,** John Street. Don't be fooled by the rather plain facade; what's inside is delightful. Rooms in the townhouse are comfortable and full of old-world charm. We stayed up the street in an extended facility that was a small, one-bedroom duplex apartment. The restaurant is well known in the area as well as in the United States. Its menu features seafood and some meat dishes. Rates for the rooms range from £50.00 to £100.00 per night and prices for dinner are approximately £15.00 or under per person. Telephone: 353-66-91-51174.

Services and Amenities

Dingle is a full-service town.

Downpatrick, Co. Down, N. Ireland

This town twenty-two miles south of Belfast isn't a priority unless you're tracing the footsteps of St. Patrick.

- **Down County Museum and St. Patrick Heritage Centre,** the Mall. Both of these facilities are housed in the eighteenth century Old County Gaol. Open mid June–mid September, Monday–Friday 11:00 A.M.–5:00 P.M., Saturday–Sunday 2:00–5:00 P.M.; mid September–mid June, Tuesday–Friday 11:00 A.M.–5:00 P.M., Saturday–Sunday 2:00–5:00 P.M. Admission is free. Telephone: 44-28-4461-5218.

Drombeg Stone Circle, Co. Cork

Ireland's most impressive prehistoric stone circle is located on the Glandore road ten miles west of Clonakilty. This circle is free and open to the public.

Dublin, Co. Dublin

This big, bustling city is home to many important sites and museums, and is a great jumping-off place for interesting day trips (see "In the Area" below).

Sites

- **Book of Kells exhibition:** "Turning Darkness Into Light," Trinity College. This exhibit showcases the Christian Celts' skill with illustrated manuscripts, and is housed in the lower level of the Old Library of Trinity College, located at the intersection of College Green and Grafton Street. Open Monday–Saturday 9:30 A.M.–5:30 P.M., Sunday 12:00–5:00 P.M. Admission: Adults £4.50. Student, child, group, and family discounts available. Telephone: 353-0-1-677-2941; fax: 353-0-1-671-9003.

- **Dublin Writers Museum,** 18 Parnell Square North. Many of Ireland's most famous writers called Dublin home. This museum was opened in 1991 in a lovely eighteenth-century townhouse and features various exhibitions chronicling the lives and works of Dublin's literary greats. There is an elegant Gallery of Writers, an excellent restaurant called the Chapter One, an inviting tea room, and a specialty bookstore that provides an out-of-print search service. Open Monday–Saturday 10:00 A.M.–5:00 P.M., Sunday 11:00 A.M.–5:00 P.M. Admission: £2.75. Telephone: 353-0-1-872-2077.

- **James Joyce Cultural Centre,** 35 N. Great George's Street. Joyce aficionados are not the only ones who will find this literary stop worth checking out. The Center is housed in a 1784 townhouse noted for its beautiful Georgian interiors. The primary display is a collection of biographies based on characters from Joyce's *Ulysses*. Open: Monday–Saturday 9:30 A.M.–5:00 P.M., Sunday 12:30–5:00 P.M. Admission: £2.75. Telephone: 353-0-1-878-8547.

- **Literary Pub Crawl** (meets at the Duke Pub, Duke Street). An entertaining introduction to some of Dublin's best-known writers and the pubs where they hung out. Operates: Easter–October 31st nightly at 7:30 P.M., Sunday 12 P.M. and 7:30 P.M.; November to Easter Thursday, Friday, and Saturday at 7:30 P.M., Sunday at 12 noon and 7:30 P.M. Closed December 20–January 5. Cost: £6.50. Purchase tickets at the Tourism Center at Suffolk Street. Telephone: 353-0-1-670-5602. Fax: 353-0-1-670-5603/454-5680. You can also inquire via e-mail (colm@dublinpubcrawl.com) or visit the Web site (www.dublinpubcrawl.com).

- **Musical Sites**

  Musical Pub Crawl: Takes guests to some of the city's must musical pubs and historical sites. Operates May 1–October 30 nightly at 7:30 P.M. Cost: £6.00. Purchase tickets at the Tourism Center at Suffolk Street. E-mail: musical. pub.crawl@officelink.eunet.it.

  Celtic Note Irish Music Store, Nassau Street: This premier music store offers a wide range of traditional, folk, ceili, and country compact discs, cassettes, and videos, music literature, and traditional musical instruments. Telephone: 353-0-1-670-4157; fax: 353-0-1-670-4158.

  "Rock n Stroll Dublin's Music Trail; Pubs, Restaurants, Night Life, and Music." This helpful booklet is available at the Dublin Tourism Office on Suffolk Street.

- **St. Patrick's Cathedral,** Patrick Street, Dublin. A magnificent and historically important church located on the site where Patrick is said to have baptized early converts. Open May and September–October, Monday–Friday 9:00 A.M.–6:00 P.M., Saturday 9:00 A.M.–5:00 P.M., Sunday 9:30 A.M.–3:00 P.M. and 4:15–5:15 P.M; June–August, Monday–Friday

9:00 A.M.–6:00 P.M., Saturday 9:00 A.M.–4:00 P.M., Sunday 9:30 A.M.–3:00 P.M. and 4:15–5:15 P.M; November–April, Monday–Friday 9:00 A.M.–6:00 P.M., Saturday 9:00 A.M.–4:00 P.M., Sunday 10:00–11:00 A.M. and 12:30–3:00 P.M. Admission: £2. Telephone: 353-0-1-475-4817.

Arriving in Dublin

If you are picking up a rental car from the airport, ask directions for exiting the terminal and follow signs to the city center. Parking is a challenge unless you are staying at a hotel where parking is provided.

If you are not driving into the city, buses operate every ten minutes in front of the airport at the stand marked Bus-Rail. The cost is £3 per person. Taxis are readily available and cost approximately £15.

Lodging

A wide range of accommodations are available in and around Dublin. We have listed a few from differing price ranges.

- **The Westbury,** Grafton Street. Elegant luxury, 203-room hotel with all the amenities of an upscale establishment. The location is also excellent, just a short block off one of Dublin's businest shopping streets. Major credit cards accepted. Rate for standard double room is approximately £215.00 per night; weekend rate for standard double is £160.00 per night. Telephone: 353-0-1-679-1122; fax: 353-0-1-679-7078.

- **Grafton Plaza,** Johnson's Place. A convenient location near Grafton Street, this seventy-five-room Georgian hotel offers neat and tasteful rooms. Major credit cards accepted. Rates for a standard double are from £100–£150 per night. Telephone: 353-0-1-475-0888.

- **Number 31,** 31 Leeson Close. This charming B&B provides a quiet respite just a short walk from St. Stephen's
Green in the center of Georgian Dublin. Noel and Deirdre
Comer are welcoming and engaging hosts who will make
you feel right at home from the moment you arrive. Most
major credit cards accepted; recently expanded to include
twenty rooms all ensuite; rate for doubles is from £94 to
£100 March through November. Telephone: 353-0-1-676-
5011; fax: 353-0-1-676-2929.

- **Jury's Christchurch Inn,** Christchurch Place. This functional hotel is a great find for the traveler looking for a convenient location and a very reasonable rate. The attached car
park is another plus. While not fancy, all rooms are ensuite,
clean, and equipped with the usual hotel amenities—phone,
TV, bathtub, and room service. Major credit cards accepted;
rates for doubles are approximately £62.00 per night. Telephone: 353-0-1-454-0010; fax: 353-0-1-454-0012.

Dining

Dublin, like any big city, offers a dizzying number of culinary choices. One of the best ways to match your desire of
the moment with the perfect restaurant is to ask for recommendations from your hotel staff or your B&B hosts. These
folks stay current on restaurant management changes and new
places that have recently opened.

We've listed some of the long-established and well-known
restaurants as well as a nice little spot we found while wandering around one night.

- **Thornton's,** 1 Portobello Road. This rather formal French
restaurant is a twenty-minute walk or short drive from St.
Stephen's Green. Considered one of Ireland's best restaurants, Thornton's understated ambience is the perfect place
to enjoy gourmet delicacies. Prices are over £25 per person.
Reservations a must. Telephone: 353-0-1-454-9067.

- **The Grey Door,** 23 Upper Pembroke Street. The Grey Door's logo fits right in with travelers on Celtic Journeys: Celtic circles representative of Neolithic tombs. This former Russo-Scandinavian restaurant has been completely transformed into an Irish establishment from the Irish-crafted decor to the items on the menu. Prices are approximately £20 to £25 per person. In the basement, a less expensive restaurant, Pier 32, offers live music most evenings. Prices are generally under £20. Telephone for both: 353-0-1-676-3286.

- **La Stampa,** 35 Dawson Street. Neoclassical style and an international menu add to the lively atmosphere here. Conveniently located between Trinity College and St. Stephen's Green, this spot offers a creative menu and fine service. Prices are approximately £20 to £25. Telephone: 353-0-1-677-8611.

- **Eden,** Meeting House Square. In a city with few outdoor eating opportunities, Eden's has a patio as well as an indoor dining room with a high wall of glass overlooking one of the main squares in Temple Bar. An eclectic menu offers vegetarian and nonvegetarian dishes. Prices are generally under £20. Telephone: 353-0-1-670-5372.

- **Al's Italian Restaurant,** 11 Andrew Street. We stumbled across this small Italian restaurant and were delighted with our find. Traditional Italian dishes including pizza provide a break from Irish meals at reasonable prices. The atmosphere is pleasant and casual. Prices are generally under £10.00 per person.

- **Bewley's Cafe,** 78-79 Grafton Street. Bewley's is a well-known name in Ireland as a purveyor of distinctive teas and coffees. As you enter the cafe you pass through a pastry shop with cases filled with sumptuously tempting delicacies. You can purchase to go or pick a table and enjoy breakfast, lunch, dinner, or a late-evening dessert. This is a great place to satisfy a sweet tooth after dinner and a stroll through center-city Dublin.

- **Pubs.** Dublin has pubs on almost every street, which are great places for inexpensive meals almost any time of day. In the evening, usually around 9:00–10:00 P.M., many of them have musicians playing traditional Irish music. For a full list of music pubs, stop in at the Dublin Tourism Centre.

Shopping

The major shopping areas in center-city Dublin are all within easy walking distance of each other. Walk along Nassau Street and Grafton Street and you will find all of the traditional Irish goods available at export prices (for VAT tax refund information, see General Information). Smaller streets going off from Grafton are full of speciality shops that serve to widen your choices of crystal, pottery, china, woolen goods, Irish linen, traditional jewelry, and books about Ireland.

Services and Amenities

Dublin is a full-service city with facilities to meet all your needs. One of the best places to get a sense of just what is offered is the Dublin Tourism Centre on Suffolk Street. This mecca of information is housed in an old church, so be sure to look closely or you'll be deceived by the exterior.

Inside you'll find a very efficient system for answering any questions you might have. Take a number from the dispensing machine near the front door on the edge of the large gift area. Then your number will appear in a display box when a consultant is available to help you. You can look through the gifts, books, and brochures while waiting for your number to appear. Then you will receive individual attention that will prove very helpful in planning your time in Dublin. Visit them on the Web at www.visitdublin.com.

In the Area

All of these cities, sites, or attractions, which are described elsewhere in this section, can be reached from Dublin:

- **Glendalough,** Co. Wicklow
- **Hill of Slane,** Co. Meath
- **Hill of Tara,** Co. Meath
- **Kells,** Co. Meath
- **Mellifont Abbey,** Co. Meath
- **Monasterboice,** Co. Meath
- **Newgrange,** Co. Meath
- **St. Brigid's Cathedral,** Kildare, Co. Kildare
- **Browne's Hill Dolmen,** Co. Carlow

Dun Aengus, Inishmore, Aran Islands, Co. Galway

See listing for Aran Islands.

Dunbeg Fort, Ventry, Dingle Peninsula, Co. Kerry

See listing for Dingle.

Dysert O'Dea, Co. Clare

See listing for Ennis.

Ennis, Co. Clare

Ennis is a convenient stop between the west and the south-west. It's the county town of Co. Clare and known for its love of traditional music and step dancing. You'll find it a good base to explore the surrounding area which includes the spectacular Cliffs of Moher and the unusual limestone plateau of the Burren.

Sites

- **Dysert O'Dea,** six miles north of Ennis. The ruins of this monastic site founded by St. Tola are somewhat overgrown, but the site includes a Romanesque doorway, a twelfth-century high cross, and the nearby remains of two stone forts.

- **Ennis Friary,** Abbey Street. One of the town's main attractions, this Franciscan friary is noted for its beautiful carvings and chancel tombs. Open daily May–September. Telephone: 353-65-22464.

- **Poulnabrone Dolmen,** north of Ennis. This impressive portal tomb dates back to 2500–2000 B.C. and is worth a stop. It is conveniently located near the Burren and the Cliffs of Moher. Admittance to this dolmen is free and always accessible.

Location

Ennis is located twenty-three miles northwest of Limerick and eighty-six miles north of Tralee.

Traveling to Ennis

If you are driving from the southwest to Ennis, go to the coastal town of Tarbert, eighteen miles north of Listowel, and take the car ferry to Killimer. The ferry runs every half hour and takes about fifteen minutes. It will save you about eighty-five miles. No reservations are needed. For more information, call the Killimer-Tarbert Ferries. Telephone: 353-65-53124; e-mail: sferry@iol.it.

Lodging

Because Ennis is a popular location, there are dozens of B&Bs to choose from. Here we have listed two more upscale establishments for those who would rather try a hotel at this stop.

- **Carnelly House,** Clarecastle. This elegant redbrick house is three miles south of Ennis and ten miles from the Shannon Airport. It sits on a one-hundred-acre estate and has large bedrooms. Gourmet dinners are also available. All five rooms are ensuite. MasterCard and Visa accepted. Rates are generally over £140.00 per room per night. Telephone: 353-65-28442; fax: 353-65-29222.

- **Old Ground,** Ennis town center. This hotel has an old-world elegance even after expansions and additions. It has a restaurant and bar and is conveniently located in the center of town. Major credit cards accepted. All fifty-eight rooms are ensuite. Rates are from approximately £100.00 to £140.00 per room per night. Telephone: 353-65-28127; fax: 353-65-28112.

Dining

Ennis has numerous restaurants and pubs. Check with your lodging host for recommendations.

Shopping

The shopper will enjoy the selection of specialty shops available in Ennis that carry good selections of Belleek china, Waterford crystal, Donegal china, Lladro, Hummel, and other collectibles. Sweaters and designer knitwear also grace the aisles of several shops.

Gallarus Oratory, Dingle Peninsula, Co. Kerry

See listing for Dingle.

Galway, Co. Galway

Galway is a delight. Small enough to reflect rural charm and large enough to offer the best of city life, Galway is the center of the regions of the west. This is a perfect base from which to explore the Aran Islands, the Burren region, and the Connemara area. Or, if you just want to walk the streets of this enchanting city, spend a few days here and relax.

Sites

• **Aran Islands.** See listing for Aran Islands.

• **Kenny's Bookshop & Art Gallery,** High Street. Ireland is a country full of books and bookstores, but family-run Kenny's is an exceptional treat. Its collection of books on Ireland, Irish history, and Irish literature can't be beat, and its selection of used and rare books offers many unusual treats. The store also has an art gallery featuring many high-quality works. Kenny's also ships overseas, and offers a unique parcel program that lets readers sign up for regular shipments of books in their areas of interest. Telephone: 353-91-562-739; fax: 353-91-568-544; Web site: www.kennys.it; e-mail: desi@kennys.it.

Location

Galway City is 136 miles west of Dublin and sixty-five miles north of Limerick.

Lodging

- **Great Southern Hotel,** Eyre Square. This beautiful, upscale hotel is right in the middle of Galway City. It offers all the amenities you would expect and the added plus of an indoor, heated swimming pool on the rooftop. All 112 rooms are ensuite. All major credit cards accepted. Rates range from £125.00 to £140.00 per room per night. Telephone: 353-91-564-041; fax: 353-91-566-704; Web site: www.gsh.it.

- **Ardilaun House,** Taylors Hill. Located in a quiet suburb, the Ardilaun House is a short five-minute drive from the center of town. This is a full-service hotel with ninety ensuite rooms that have been recently refurbished. Major credit cards accepted. Prices range from £100.00 to £140.00 per room per night. Telephone: 353-91-521-433; fax: 353-91-521-546; Web site: www.commerce.it/ardilaun; e-mail: ardilaun@iol.it.

- **Park House Hotel,** Forster Street. This hotel is very conveniently located just one block off of Eyre Square in the center of town. We have stayed here several times and enjoyed both the amenities and the service. Full service hotel. Major credit cards accepted. Rates range from £80.00 to £115.00 per room per night. Telephone: 353-91-564-924; fax: 353-91-569-219; e-mail: parkhousehotel@tinet.it.

Dining

Galway is a diner's delight with a wide range of excellent restaurants and pubs. We've listed just a few that are our choices for a lovely evening meal.

- **The Park Room Restaurant,** Park House Hotel. This award-winning restaurant offers an imaginative gourmet menu in the warm ambience of a tastefully decorated dining room. Prices are approximately £30.00 per person for a full meal. Telephone: 353-91-564-924.

- **K. C. Blakes Brasserie,** Quay Street. Casual dining, a modern interior, and a stone exterior add to the charm of this restaurant conveniently located on bustling Quay Street. Prices are approximately £15.00–£20.00 per person for a full meal. Telephone: 353-91-561-826.

Shopping

Galway is full of wonderful shops that carry all the traditional Irish goods anyone could desire. It is also the home of the Claddagh ring, named after a former Irish-speaking fishing village just outside the city of Galway. This design of two hands clasped around a heart with a crown above it is available all over Ireland. If you haven't purchased one yet, this might be a good place to decide if this is a treasure you want to take home.

One long shopping street winds through the center of town and changes names four times: William Street, Shop Street, High Street, and Quay Street. Side streets are also full of opportunities to browse or buy.

- **Claddagh Jewellers,** Eyre Square. Beautiful jewelry shop with a wide range of all kinds of jewelry as well as Claddagh items. Telephone: 353-91-563-282; fax: 353-91-566-615.

- **Galway Irish Crystal Heritage Centre,** Merling Park, Dublin Road. You can enjoy a guided heritage tour and see how Galway Irish crystal is made, then browse through the gift shop and showroom. There is also a restaurant overlooking Galway Bay. Telephone: 353-91-757-311; fax: 353-91-757-316.

- **Royal Tara China Visitor Centre,** Tara Hall, Mervue. Only minutes outside of the city, Royal Tara China offers tours, a showroom and gift shop, and a tea room. Telephone: 353-91-751-301; fax: 353-91-757-574; Web site: www.Royal-Tara.it.

Services and Amenities

Galway is a full-service town. The Tourist Information Office is located on Victoria Place, one block off of Eyre Square. Telephone: 353-91-563-081; fax: 353-91-565-201.

Glendalough, Co. Wicklow

This is, hands down, our favorite mainland monastic site. The setting is beautiful and offers some unbelievably restful walking trails. The monastic remains are among the most impressive in all of Ireland. Even the visitors center is one of the best, although you don't have to go through the center to access the grounds. In short, don't miss Glendalough. And while you're in the area, you can enjoy a drive through the Wicklow Mountains National Park just west of Glendalough.

- **Glendalough Visitor's Center.** The visitor's center is adjacent to the monastic ruins and is an excellent place to begin your exploration of Glendalough ruins and lakes. Open mid October–mid March, daily 9:30 A.M.–5:00 P.M.; mid March–through May, daily 9:30 A.M.–6:00 P.M.; June–August, daily 9:00 A.M.–6:30 P.M.; September–mid October, daily 9:30 A.M.–6:00 P.M. Admission: free with Heritage Card; adults ₤2.00, children ₤1.00. Senior citizen, family, and group discounts available. Telephone: 353-404-45325; fax: 353-404-45626.

Location

Glendalough is located thirty-four miles south of Dublin. The villages of Laragh and Rathdrum are adjacent to the village of Glendalough and the monastic site of Glendalough.

Lodging

Several lovely B&Bs are nestled in this peaceful valley. We have stayed several times in the Derrybawn House, listed below, and have loved it. We've also included the Glendalough Hotel in this listing. We have enjoyed a stay in this quaint hotel that borders the valley, allowing guests to walk right out the hotel door and onto the many hiking trails, ruins, and lakeside paths that make this valley so idyllic.

- **The Derrybawn House,** Rathdrum. This beautiful home was rebuilt in the nineteenth century after being burnt down during the 1798 Rising. Gardens and meadows surround the house and provide the traveler with a peaceful rest only one mile away from Glendalough and just several hundred feet from the Laragh intersection. All six rooms are ensuite and some are furnished with impressive antiques. The formal dining room houses displays of lovely china and silver and ensures a feast for the eyes as well as the stomach. No credit cards are accepted. Rates are approximately £30.00 per person per night. Telephone: 353-404-45134; fax: 353-404-45109.

- **The Glendalough Hotel,** Glendalough. This family-run hotel is right next to the entrance to the Glendalough monastic ruins. It is an ideal location for touring the Glendalough valley and has all the amenities of a moderate hotel. All forty-four rooms have telephones, TV, and are ensuite. Rates range from £35.00 to £47.00 per person per night. Telephone: 353-404-45135; fax: 353-404-45142.

Dining

- **Wicklow Heather,** Laragh. This quaint cottage restaurant serves hearty portions of traditional Irish dishes at moderate prices. It is located on the main road between Glendalough and Laragh and offers indoor and outdoor seating, weather permitting. Prices range from £7.00 to £13.00 per person for a full meal.

Shopping

While shops are limited in this tiny village, there is a very nice and reasonably priced woolen mill outlet store.

- **The Woollen Mills at Glendalough.** Located 500 yards outside Laragh village on the Rathdrum road, this store is a pleasant shopping experience and a great place to pick out an Irish sweater from their large selection. Open daily from 9:30 A.M–5:00 P.M. Telephone: 353-404-45156.

Services and Amenities

These small villages provide for the traveler's basic needs. Gas stations and a convenience store are available. For further information, you can contact the Tourist Information Office for Co. Wicklow. Telephone: 353-404-69117; fax: 353-404-69118.

Grey Abbey, Co. Down, N. Ireland

Grey Abbey is located in Greyabbey village on the west side of the Ards peninsula, eighteen miles east of Belfast. Open April–September, Tuesday–Sunday.

Grianan Aileach Fort, Burt, Inishowen Peninsula, Co. Donegal

One of Ireland's best preserved Iron Age forts, Grianan Aileach, located on the Inishowen peninsula of Co. Donegal in the Republic of Ireland, is only three miles east of Derry in Co. Londonderry, Northern Ireland.

Near the base of the hill leading to the fort is a beautiful visitors center and restaurant housed in an old stone church. The restaurant is stylish and suitable for a lovely evening meal. The displays and exhibits at the Grianan Aileach visitors center tell the story of the ancient fort with the use of life-size wax figures set in scenes representative of the culture of the time. Open in summer, daily 10:00 A.M.–6:00 P.M.; restaurant open daily from 10:00 A.M.–10:00 P.M.; winter, daily 12:00–6:00 P.M.; restaurant open daily from 12:00–10:00 P.M. Admission: £2.00, family £5.00.

Gweedore, Co. Donegal

If you're a Celtic music buff, tiny Gweedore has a unique appeal.

Leo's Tavern is the pub where the Irish band Clannad (made up of Leo's children and other relatives) got its start, and the Ostan Gweedore Hotel is quite comfortable—if not ostentatious.

Hill of Slane, Co. Meath

Just north of the town of Slane, the Hill of Slane is an important site where St. Patrick denounced pagan celebrations. It features nice ruins which are free and open to the public.

The town of Slane, just south of the Hill of Slane and twenty-nine miles northwest of Dublin, is a lovely Georgian village. This is a pleasant spot to stop for lunch while touring the area. The Conyngham Arms Hotel, located at the cross-roads of the village, serves a buffet from 12–3:00 P.M. and a bar menu all day.

Hill of Tara, Co. Meath

The Hill of Tara is steeped in Irish history. Standing over three hundred feet above sea level, it affords a panoramic view of the Boyne Valley, the central Irish plains, and, on a clear day, the mountains east of Galway. It is twenty-one miles northwest of Dublin and ten miles south of Navan. Begin your visit at the Interpretative Center, housed in a charming old Church of Ireland sanctuary. Open May–mid June, daily 10:00 A.M.–5:00 P.M.; mid June–mid September, daily 9:30 A.M.–6:30 P.M.; mid September through October, daily 10:00 A.M.–5:00 P.M. Admission: free with Heritage Card; adults £1.50, children £0.60. Senior citizen, family, and group discounts available. Telephone 353-46-25903; fax: 353-01-25903.

After climbing the gently sloping hillside and exploring Stone Age and Iron Age ruins, enjoy a tea break in Mike Maguire's Gift Shoppe located at the base of the hill. The scones are delicious and the shop offers many traditional Irish gifts.

Inishbofin, Co. Galway

This beautiful, historic island is located about six and a half miles off the Northwest coast of Connemara. Kings Ferries operates out of Cleggan, near the city of Clifden. Telephone: 353-95-44642; fax: 353-95-44327; Web site: www.failte.con/cleggan/; e-mail: conamara@indigo.it.

Inisheer, Aran Islands, Co. Galway

See listing for Aran Islands.

Inishmaan, Aran Islands, Co. Galway

See listing for Aran Islands.

Inishmore, Aran Islands, Co. Galway

See listing for Aran Islands.

Inishmurray, Co. Galway

This island may be reached by ferry from Rosses Point.

Isle of Iona, Argyll, Scotland

Perhaps the most important historic Celtic monastic site, Iona is now home to a vibrant Christian community. This island also has many sites related to St. Columba.

Location

The Isle of Iona is part of the Inner Hebridean chain of islands and is located off the far western tip of the Isle of Mull. The Isle of Mull is located off the west coast of Scotland near the town of Oban.

Travel to Iona

While arranging travel to Iona appears a bit complicated, it is actually a very pleasant trip once you have deciphered the schedules of the various modes of transportation. We suggest that you plan to stay the night in the town of Oban, Scotland, before going to Iona.

It is possible to travel to Iona and back to Oban in one day, but you will wish you'd planned for more time. We stayed for one night on Iona and would have loved to linger longer.

From Oban to Iona you begin with a ferry crossing from Oban to Craignure on the Isle of Mull. This is a car ferry but if you are going on to Iona and not stopping over on Mull, leave your car in Oban. The hotel we list in Oban will allow you to do so for free.

At the pier on Mull you take a scheduled bus from Craignure to Fionnphort. Then you take another short ferry ride from Fionnphort to Iona. The entire round-trip costs approximately £16.00 per person. If you take a car on the ferry it is £40.00, returning the same day.

While in Fionnphort you may want to take some time to stop at the Saint Columba Exhibition. Open Monday–Saturday 10:00 A.M.–6:00 P.M., Sunday 11:00 A.M.–6:00 P.M. Telephone: 44-1681-700-660; fax: 44-1681-700-640.

Since ferry and bus schedules change, the best plan is to call the ferry company (Caledonian MacBrayne Ferry Company) a few days before arrival and determine the ferry schedule that will hook up with the bus and the remaining ferry. It really is much easier than it sounds. Telephone: 44-1631-566-688; Web site: www.calmac.co.uk.

The entire travel time from Oban to Iona is about two hours.

Arriving on Iona

If you are staying overnight, you can call your hotel or B&B and they will send a car down to pick you and your luggage up. We brought only a small bag each and were able to walk to our hotel.

Lodging

There are a few B&Bs on Iona but we opted for and really enjoyed the St. Columba Hotel, listed below. The best place for current B&B information is the Oban Tourist Board. Telephone: 44-1631-563-122.

- **St. Columba Hotel,** Isle of Iona, Argyll, Scotland. This hotel is ideally located near the geographical center of the island and right next to St. Mary's Cathedral and the Iona Abbey. The rooms are simple in decor, spotless, and many have wonderful views of the Sound of Iona. There is an inviting sun room where guests congregate all during the day and evening. A full dinner is served in the dining room, which is probably the best option for dining on the island. There are fourteen rooms with twin beds, four doubles, and nine singles, all ensuite. Prices are approximately £54.00 per person per night including breakfast and dinner. Telephone: 44-1681-700-304; fax: 44-1681-700-688.

- **Religious Communities: The Iona Community** is located at the Iona Abbey, next to the Columba Hotel. The Community offers several options for visitors to stay with them.

From March through December, they hold weeklong programs with various spiritual themes. Some of these are open to the public, some are not. Guests may participate in community activities, which include meals, daily worship, program activities, chores, and social events. The accommodations are simple, mostly rooms with bunk beds, four twin-bedded rooms, one three-person room, and one five-person room. If visitors do not choose to stay for the weeklong program, they may stay for a minimum of three nights with arrival on Saturday or Tuesday. The Community is closed to visitors in January and February. For more information, write The Iona Community, Isle of Iona, Argyll, PA76 6SN, Scotland; telephone: 44-1681-700-404; fax: 44-1681-700-460. There is also a Catholic House of Prayer on Iona.

- **In Oban: Dungallan House Hotel,** Gallanach Road, Oban, Argyll, Scotland. This beautiful Scottish Victorian house is perched on a hill overlooking Oban Bay. The proprietors, George and Janice Stewart, are known for the wonderful evening meals they serve. Rooms are clean, comfortable, and tastefully decorated. One of the greatest reasons to stay is its closeness to Iona. You can leave your car here overnight and it is an easy, though hilly, walk to the ferry depot. Taxi service is available as well. Major credit cards accepted. Prices: £70.00 per room per night. Telephone: 44-1631-563-799; fax: 44-1631-566-711.

Dining

- **St. Columba Hotel,** listed on the preceding page.

Shopping

Several small craft shops specializing in local pottery dot the island. The Abbey has a gift shop that offers a number of local goods as well as numerous books about Iona. There is another rare bookshop across from the St. Columba Hotel and a local pottery shop across from the Abbey where you can see artisans making their wares.

Kinsale, Co. Cork

This charming little seaside town is rich in history and a convenient jumping off place for touring the coastal sites between here and Bantry, Co. Cork.

Sites

- **Timoleague Abbey.** See listing for Timoleague Abbey.
- **Drombeg Stone Circle.** See listing for Drombeg Stone Circle.

Location

Kinsale is located eighteen miles southwest of Cork.

Lodging

There are a number of B&Bs and small hotels. We've listed one of each, including The Lighthouse, where we especially enjoyed our hostess, Carmel.

- **The Lighthouse,** the Rock. On a hill just above the town center, this cozy and comfortable B&B is a fun and interesting place to spend a night. The highlight is the vivacious owner, Carmel Kelly-O'Gorman. Her home is full of antiques and history which she colorfully shares with guests. Some theme rooms add to the fun, like the Out of Africa room. All five rooms are ensuite. Major credit cards accepted. Rates are from £30.00 to £35.00 per person per night. Telephone: 353-21-477-2734; fax: 353-21-477-3282.

- **The Blue Haven,** 3–4 Pearse Street. This quaint hotel is right in the middle of the town. Rooms are recently refurbished and all 18 are ensuite. Major credit cards accepted. Rates are from £50.00 to £100.00 per room per night. Telephone: 353-21-477-2209; fax: 353-21-477-268; e-mail: bluhaven @iol.it.

Dining

Since Kinsale is often referred to as the gourmet capital of Ireland, you'll enjoy a good selection of dining experiences. Check with your B&B or hotel host for suggestions.

Services and Amenities

Kinsale is a full-service town. The tourist information office for Co. Cork can also provide helpful information: Telephone: 353-21-427-3251.

Kells, Co. Meath

Once home to an important monastery, Kells is now a small market town thirty-five miles northwest of Dublin. On many maps Kells is noted by its Irish name, Ceanannus Mor.

Kenmare, Co. Kerry

Kenmare is a bustling town located on the southeast side of the Ring of Kerry road. Tour buses abound and the town is worth a brief stop. Lots of pleasant and convenient restaurants line the streets around the central town park.

Kenmare is famous for its traditional lace which was originally introduced by nuns from the local convent during the convent years. Shoppers will find many delights in numerous stores. Be sure to check out Quills Woolen Market adjacent to the park.

Site

- **Kenmare Circle.** This small but impressive stone circle is located just outside the town.

Killarney, Co. Kerry

While Killarney is one of the more commercialized parts of Ireland, it is also a beautiful area dotted with mountains and lakes. While traveling through Celtic Ireland, Killarney is a good base from which to make day trips to the Ring of Kerry and the Dingle Peninsula.

We have also listed options for staying in Cahirciveen, Ring of Kerry, and Dingle Town, Dingle Peninsula, but here's a brief rundown on Killarney if you choose to make your home base there.

Sites

- **Dunbeg Fort,** Dingle Peninsula. See listing for Dingle.
- **Gallarus Oratory,** Dingle Peninsula. See listing for Dingle.
- **Kenmare Circle,** Ring of Kerry. See listing for Kenmare Circle.
- **Skellig Michael,** Ring of Kerry. See listing for Skellig Michael.
- **Staigue Fort,** Ring of Kerry. See listing for Staigue Fort.

Location

Killarney is located fifty-four miles west of Cork City.

Lodging

In the areas around Killarney town proper there are the expected large number of B&Bs. Here we've listed some hotels in or near the town.

- **Hotel Europe,** Killorglin Road, Fossa. This five-star resort is located five minutes from town and offers many amenities including two restaurants, two bars, pool, sauna, tennis court, horseback riding, fishing, and bicycles. All major credit cards accepted. All 205 rooms are ensuite. Rates are from £100.00 to £150.00 per room per night. Telephone: 353-64-31900; fax: 353-64-32118.

- **Killarney Park Hotel,** Kenmare Place. This hotel is conveniently located in the center of town and offers modern, tastefully decorated rooms. All major credit cards accepted. All sixty-seven rooms are ensuite. Rates are from £100.00 to £150.00 per room per night. Telephone: 353-64-35555; fax: 353-64-35266.

- **Royal Hotel,** College Street. This traditional hotel is a short walk from city center. Major credit cards are accepted. There are forty-nine rooms, all ensuite. Rates are from £50.00 to £100.00 per room per night. Telephone: 353-64-31853; fax: 353-64-34001.

Dining

- **Gaby's Seafood,** 17 High Street. This popular spot is considered the best seafood restaurant in town. Prices are from £25.00 to £50.00 per person for a three-course meal. Telephone: 353-64-32519.

- **Dingle's Restaurant,** 40 New Street. Many locals as well as travelers enjoy the warm atmosphere at this town-center restaurant. Prices are from £15.00 to £25.00 per person for a three-course meal. Telephone: 353-64-31079.

- **Sheila's,** 75 High Street. Simple Irish dishes that have enticed travelers for more than thirty years make Sheila's a friendly dining spot a good find with good value for the money. Prices are under £15.00 per person. Telephone: 353-64-31270.

Shopping

The main shopping streets in Killarney are Main Street and High Street. From crafts and souvenirs to crystal and woolens, the shopper will find much to choose from on the streets of Killarney.

Services and Amenities

Killarney is a full-service town. The Tourist Information Board is located in the Town Hall on Main Street. Telephone: 353-64-31633.

Knock, Co. Mayo

The town of Knock is located about seventy-four miles north of Galway. It is the site of the Basilica of Our Lady, a modern basilica and Marian shrine. This pilgrimage site is visited by 1.5 million people every year. The Basilica is open all year. Shrine open May–October daily; November–April by appointment. Telephone: 353-94-88100; fax: 353-94-88295. Telephone for the Knock Tourist Information: 353-94-88193.

Kylemore Abbey, Co. Galway

This is a beautiful spot to take a lunch break and enjoy Kylemore Abbey's peaceful surroundings as you travel from Galway to the Westport area. Adjacent to the Abbey is a large and generously stocked gift shop and charming tea room. Open March–November, daily 10:00 A.M.–6:00 P.M.; February–December, daily 9:30 A.M.–6:00 P.M. Admission is free. Telephone: 353-95-41146.

Limerick, Co. Limerick

Limerick is located 123 miles southwest of Dublin. Frank McCourt put Limerick on Ireland's literary map and the spots made famous in *Angela's Ashes* are now part of the local tourist industry. There is an *Angela's Ashes* Tour that takes place daily at 2:30 P.M. from the tourist office in Arthur's Quay. Tourist Information Office: telephone: 353-61-317-522; fax: 353-61-317-939. For additional tour information, contact Noel Curtin, Shannonside Tours. Telephone: 353-61-311-935; e-mail: shannonsidetours@tinet.it.

Listowel, Co. Kerry

For those with literary interests, Listowel hosts a writing festival which has been held annually for over twenty-five years. Web site: www.kerryweb.it; e-mail: writers@tinet.it.

This small market town is located sixteen miles northwest of Tralee. It is well known in the area for its annual horse race held on the third week in September, which results in traffic being snarled to a snail's pace for those just passing through.

Lower Lough Erne, Co. Fermanagh, N. Ireland

There are three interesting monastic sites in this lake:

- **Boa Island,** east of Belleek on the north side of the lake. It is accessible by car.

- **Devinish Island,** near the southern tip of the lake, can be reached by ferry from Trory Point or by ferry or waterbus from Enniskillen.

- **White Island,** located on the northeast side of the lake, can be reached by boat from the Castle Archdale marina.

For ferry information, call Erne Tours at 44-28-6632-2882.

Monasterboice, Co. Louth

This monastic site has some of Ireland's most impressive Celtic stone crosses as well as a few remains.

Monasterboice is located five miles north of Drogheda and eleven miles northeast of Slane. It is open daily and admission is free.

Mellifont Abbey, Co. Louth

This abbey, which played an important role in Ireland's monastic reform, has some nice ruins.

A small museum adjacent to the car park displays exhibits that depict the history and building of the abbey. Open May–mid June, daily 10:00 A.M.–5:00 P.M.; June–mid September, daily 9:30 A.M.–6:30 P.M.; mid September–mid October, 10:00 A.M.–5:00 P.M. Admission: free with Heritage Card; adults £1.50, children £0.60. Senior citizen, family, and group discounts available. Telephone: 353-41-982-6459.

Navan Fort, Co. Armagh

See listing for Armagh.

Nendrum, Mahee Island, Strangford Lough, Co. Down, N. Ireland

This is one of the earliest and most thoroughly excavated Irish monasteries. Mahee Island is located in Strangford Lough, sixteen miles east of Belfast.

Newgrange, Knowth, and Dowth, Co. Meath

A visit to Newgrange, one of the most significant passage graves in Europe, begins at the Bru na Boinne Visitor Centre, five miles east of Slane. This beautiful and informative center includes interpretive displays, tours of Newgrange and Knowth, as well as a gift shop and delightful tea room. Open March–April, daily 9:30 A.M.–5:30 P.M.; May, daily 9:00 A.M.–6:30 P.M.;

June–mid September, daily 9:00 A.M.–7:00 P.M.; mid September through end of September, daily 9:00 A.M.–6:30 P.M.; October, daily 9:30 A.M.–5:30 P.M.; November–February, daily 9:30 A.M.–5:00 P.M. Admission: free with Heritage Card; adults £2 to £5, children £1 to £2.25. Senior citizen, family, and group discounts available. Telephone: 353-41-982-4488. This is a very busy site and delays may occur during the summer months.

Piper's Stones, Co. Wicklow

Remote and run-down, this is not Ireland's most impressive circle. Still, if you're in the vicinity, it might make an exciting challenge trying to find it.

Poulnabrone Dolmen, Co. Clare

See listing under Ennis.

Rock of Cashel, Cashel, Co. Tipperary

This attractive site, which sits upon a commanding hill, has been an important place in Ireland's religious and political history. Open mid September–mid March, daily 9:00 A.M.–4:30 P.M.; mid March–mid June, daily 9:00 A.M.–5:30 P.M.; mid June–mid September, daily 9:00 A.M.–7:30 P.M. Admission: free with Heritage Card; adults £3.00, children £1.25. Senior citizen, family, and group discounts available. Telephone: 353-62-61437; fax: 353-62-62988. This is a very busy site and delays may occur during the summer.

St. Brigid's Cathedral, Co. Kildare

Dedicated to Ireland's most beloved female saint, who founded an early monastery on the site, St. Brigid's Cathedral is located right in the middle of the town of Kildare, which grew up around the religious center. Open daily 10:00 A.M.– 6:00 P.M. Admission is free.

St. Enda's Monastery, Inishmore, Aran Islands, Co. Galway

See listing for Aran Islands.

St. Patrick's Cathedral

There are three significant churches named after the patron saint of Ireland:

- **St. Patrick's Protestant Cathedral,** Dublin—see listing for Dublin.

- **St. Patrick's Protestant Cathedral,** Armagh, N. Ireland— see listing for Armagh.

- **St. Patrick's Catholic Cathedral,** Armagh, N. Ireland— see listing for Armagh.

St. Patrick's Purgatory, Station Island, Lough Derg, Co. Donegal

This site has been an important destination for Christian pilgrims from the days of Celtic Christianity to our own day. Lough Derg, located on Station Island, is twenty miles east of Donegal and then five miles north of the village of Pettigo. But don't attempt to visit if you haven't registered for one of the center's events. Only pilgrims may go to the island, but other visitors to the area can go to the departure jetty, soak up the atmosphere, and view the island basilica from across the lake.

Scattery Island, Co. Clare

An early Celtic island monastery situated in the estuary of the River Shannon, Scattery is accessible by boat from Kilrush, five and a half miles west of the Tarbert Ferry landing at Killimer.

Skellig Michael, Co. Kerry

Simply put, this rocky island, once home to an intrepid group of solitude-seeking monks, is one of the world's most stunning spiritual sites.

Weather permitting, adventurous travelers can take a boat out to Skellig Michael, spend a few hours exploring, and return to the small harbor at Portmagee on Valentia Island (see listing for Cahirsiveen). If you're lucky, you can ride with Des Lavelle, who knows more about the island than any other living human (call 353-66-94-76124). The whole package costs about £20.00. For information on Pat Murphy's "fast" boat call 353-66-94-77156. Boats usually run May–October, weather permitting.

Sligo, Co. Sligo

Sligo, the largest town in the northwest, is situated in the midst of many megalithic sites. It is also the birthplace of W. B. Yeats, making it a good jumping-off point for touring both Celtic and literary Ireland.

Sites

- **Carrowkeel.** This is a megalithic cemetery containing many impressive tombs.
- **Carrowmore,** 8 miles south of Sligo. See listing.
- **Creevykeel.** This is a fine example of the prehistoric court tomb.
- **Tobernalt.** See listing.

Location

Sligo is eighty-six miles northeast of Galway and 135 miles northwest of Dublin. It is on the northwest coast of Sligo Bay.

Lodging

- **Sligo Park Hotel,** Pearse Road. Set in seven acres of park land just one mile outside of town on N4, this full service hotel is a pleasant and comfortable stop. Each of the 110 rooms are ensuite and have color TV, radio, and direct-dial telephones. An excellent restaurant and casual bar will meet all your culinary needs. All major credit cards accepted. Rates are approximately £90.00 to £120.00 per room per night. Telephone: 353-71-60291; fax: 353-71-69556.

Dining

There are many fine dining spots located in the area's hotels and manor houses. Check with your hotel staff for suggestions both in your hotel and elsewhere.

- **Bistro Bianconi,** 44 O'Connell Street. This lively restaurant serves Italian favorites including a large selection of pizza baked in a wood-burning oven. No lunch is served, but this is a nice stop for dinner if you want to skip Irish fare one night. Prices are generally under £15.00 per person for a full meal. Telephone: 353-71-41744.

- **Hargagon's Pub,** 4 O'Connell Street. This is a well-known Sligo pub which serves good pub food including Irish stew. Telephone: 353-71-70933.

Services and Amenities

Sligo is a full-service town with all the amenities you would expect. A good general information stop would be the Tourist Information Office at Temple and Charles Streets. It's in the

building that houses the Hawk's Well Theatre. Open Monday–
Friday 9:00 A.M.–1:00 P.M. and 2:00–5:00 P.M. Closed Saturday
and Sunday. Information is available on all of the northwest at
this office.

Staigue Fort, Castlecove, Ring of Kerry, Co. Kerry

Located two and a half miles inland at Castlecove on the Ring
of Kerry, this stone fort is a well-preserved and nicely situated
example of an Iron Age fortress.

A small but nice place to visit is the Staigue Fort Exhibition
Centre on the Ring of Kerry road at the turnoff for the Fort. It
features an artistic representation of the fort, a video presentation, and a coffee and gift shop. Open Easter–September,
daily 10:00 A.M.–9:00 P.M. Telephone: 353-66-75127.

Thoor Ballylee, Gort, Co. Galway

Nobel Prize–winning poet W. B. Yeats purchased this four-
teenth-century Norman tower in 1916 and transformed it into
a livable summer home. Located twenty-nine miles south of
Galway, it is a fun stop for Yeats fans. An audiovisual tour is
offered including readings from Yeats's poetry. Open Easter–
September, daily 10:00 A.M.–6:00 P.M. Admission: £3.00. Telephone: 353-91-631-436.

Timoleague Abbey

The ruins of this beautiful Franciscan abbey are located twelve
miles west of Kinsale. Admission is free, it is open all the time,
and the entrance gate is around the back, off the road.

Tobernalt, Co. Sligo

This ancient holy well was also the site of clandestine Catholic meetings during the harsh years of oppression. Tobernalt is located three miles south of Sligo by Lough Gill. It is free and open to the public.

Tory Island, Co. Donegal

If you're interested in Celtic monks or musicians, this isolated island might have something for you. Tory Island is off the far northwest corner of Ireland and is accessible by boat daily in the summer and in the winter when the weather permits. Boats leave from Magheraroaty Pier near Gortahork, and from Bunbeg. Telephone for boat information: Magheraroaty Pier, 353-74-35061; Bunbeg, 353-75-31991.

Westport, Co. Mayo

Westport is a delightful town with tree-lined streets and the Carrowbeg River running through the center between the North and South Mall.

If the Celtic traveler wants to climb Croagh Patrick (see listing), this is the perfect place to spend the night and relax after a strenuous day, or spend two nights to allow for an early start up the mountain. If bad weather prevents a day of climbing, Westport offers good shopping, dining, and fun pubs.

Sites

- **Croagh Patrick.** See listing for Croagh Patrick.

- **Matt Molloy's Pub.** This lively pub is owned by the flutist for the Chieftains, which makes this one of the hottest spots in town. Expect a large crowd.

Location

Westport is fifty-five miles north of Galway and five miles east of Croagh Patrick.

Lodging

Westport has a number of B&Bs in the area. We opted to stay in town so that we could conveniently travel between Croagh Patrick and the town. Our hotel of choice is listed below.

• **The Olde Railway Hotel,** the Mall. Elegant antiques adorn the public rooms of this traditional old hotel, reminding guests of its rich history. The rooms have been refurbished and offer a clean and comfortable base while visiting this area. All major credit cards accepted. All twenty-four rooms are ensuite. Rates range from £50.00 to £100.00 per room per night. Telephone: 353-98-25166; fax: 353-98-25090; Web site: http://westport.mayo-ireland.it/railway.htm; e-mail: railway@anu.it.

Dining

• **Quay Cottage,** the Quay. On several trips we've enjoyed wonderful dinners at Quay Cottage. With lots of seaside-related decor and several fireplaces, this is a fun and friendly place that also serves great food. Prices range from £12.00 to £20.00. Telephone: 353-98-26412.

Shopping

Westport is a pretty town with good shopping along Bridge Street.

- **Carraig Donn,** Bridge Street. This lovely store has its own range of knitwear and a large selection of pottery, china, and crystal. Telephone: 353-98-26287.

Services and Amenities

Westport is a full-service town. The Westport Tourist Office is located on the Mall. Telephone: 353-98-25711; fax: 353-98-26709.

12

Suggested Itineraries

If you're interested in visiting some of Ireland's many spiritual sites, the itineraries and maps on the following pages will help you plan a thorough yet realistic trip.

Dublin Day Trips

Some of Ireland's most impressive sites are located a short distance from Dublin, making this cosmopolitan city a fine place to stay.

1. Newgrange, Mellifont Abbey, Monasterboice (Co. Meath)

You will want to begin your day with a visit to the Newgrange necropolis, some fifty miles north of Dublin. Allow most of the morning for touring the site and enjoying the Bru na Boinne visitors center. This is also a good place to eat lunch before going on to Mellifont Abbey and Monasterboice.

Both of these afternoon stops can be made with short or leisurely visits. You can easily be back in Dublin by late afternoon.

Dublin Day Trips

2. Hill of Tara, Kells, Hill of Slane (Co. Meath)

These three stops are between twenty and fifty-five miles north of Dublin to the west of the sites noted in the previous itinerary. Begin with the Hill of Tara. Be sure to peek in at Mike Maguire's Gift and Tea Shoppe at the base of the hill before heading up to the town of Kells. After spending some time in Kells, drive over to the charming town of Slane, which is a good lunch stop. The Hill of Slane is right outside the town, and you will have time to wander among the ruins before going back to Dublin.

3. Glendalough (Co. Wicklow)

A visit to Glendalough deserves a full day in order to soak up the atmosphere and history and enjoy the magnificent scenery. Just thirty-four miles south of Dublin, your drive will be an easy one once you leave the Dublin city traffic.

The entrance to the Wicklow Mountain National Park is just west of Glendalough, and is a beautiful drive if time allows.

Of course, we also believe Glendalough is a wonderful place to stay for a restful night or two.

4. Kildare, Carlow (Co. Kildare, Co. Carlow)

The towns of Kildare and Carlow and the surrounding area make for an interesting touring day south of Dublin. Check the A–Z Guide in this book for information on St. Brigid's Cathedral (Kildare), Browneshill Dolmen (Carlow), and the town of Carlow for suggestions on places to visit.

5. Clonmacnois (Co. Offaly)

Travel west from Dublin approximately one hundred miles to Athlone, and then go south about thirteen miles to Clonmacnois. There is a small tea room at the site that is a convenient lunch stop.

DUBLIN TOURS

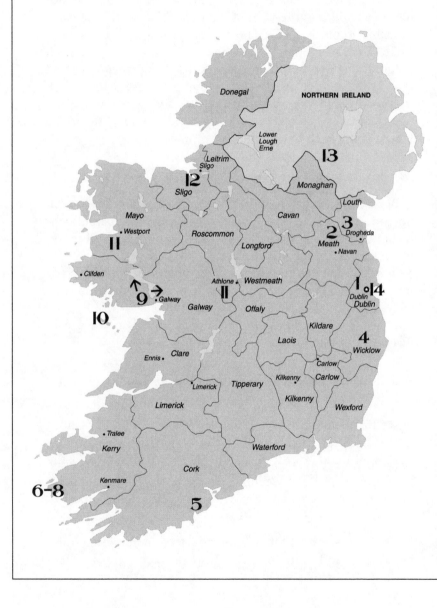

Dublin Tours

These two tours originate and terminate in Dublin. Descriptions of sites suggested are found in chapter 11, the A–Z Guide.

1. Eleven-Day Tour of the Republic of Ireland

Day 1: Arrival in Dublin (stay overnight in Dublin).

Day 2: Tour Newgrange, Mellifont Abbey, Monasterboice (stay overnight in Dublin).

Day 3: Tour Hill of Tara, Kells, Hill of Slane (stay overnight in Dublin).

Day 4: Drive to and tour Glendalough (stay overnight in Glendalough).

Day 5: Drive to Kinsale, touring along the way. Possible stops can include Kildare, Carlow, Cashel, Waterford (stay overnight in Kinsale).

Day 6: Drive to Cahirsiveen, touring along the way. Stop at Timoleague Abbey, Drombeg Stone Circle, Staigue Fort. From Kenmare you will be driving on the beautiful Ring of Kerry road (stay overnight in Cahirsiveen).

Day 7: Boat trip to Skellig Michael, weather permitting. If the weather is bad, a day trip to the Dingle Peninsula is a good option (stay overnight in Cahirsiveen).

Day 8: Boat trip to Skellig Michael if the weather was bad the day before and if the weather is good today. If you have bad weather both days, today you could drive up to Killarney or relax in the Cahirsiveen area (stay overnight in Cahirsiveen).

Day 9: Drive to Galway, touring along the way. You could drive up through Limerick or take the car ferry from Tarbert to Kilrush. Look at possible stops under Ennis in the A–Z Guide of this book (stay overnight in Galway).

Day 10: Fly or ferry to the Aran Islands and back to Galway (stay overnight in Galway).

Day 11: Return to Dublin.

2. Fourteen-Day Tour of the Republic of Ireland and Northern Ireland

Days 1 through 10 are the same as Tour 1.

Day 11: Drive from Galway to Westport, touring along the way. Stops can include Kylemore Abbey and Croagh Patrick (stay overnight in Westport).

Day 12: Drive to Sligo with a stop at the Carrowmore tombs. Read about other area sites in the A–Z Guide under "Sligo" (stay overnight in Sligo).

Day 13: Drive to Armagh, touring along the way. Stops can include St. Patrick's Purgatory (advance registration required), Lower Lough Erne, and sites listed in the A–Z Guide under Armagh (stay overnight in Armagh or Belfast).

Day 14: Return to Dublin.

West Tour

Seven-Day Tour of the West

Day 1: Arrive Shannon International Airport and drive to Ennis (stay overnight in Ennis).

Day 2: Tour the Ennis area. Stops may include Poulnabrone Dolmen, Dysert O'Dea, and Cliffs of Moher (stay overnight in Ennis).

Day 3: Drive to Galway, touring along the way. Stops may include Thoor Ballylee and the Burren (stay overnight in Galway).

Day 4: Explore the beautiful city of Galway (stay overnight in Galway).

Day 5: Fly or ferry to the Aran Islands and back to Galway (stay overnight in Galway).

Day 6: Drive to Westport, touring along the way. Stops may include Kylemore Abbey and Croagh Patrick (stay overnight in Westport).

Day 7: Return to Shannon International Airport.

WEST TOUR

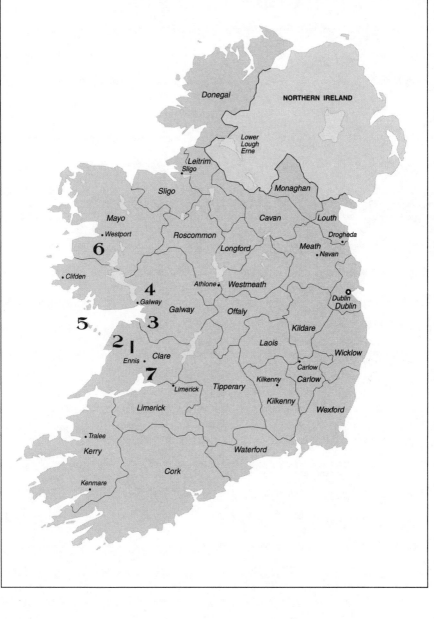

Recommended Resources

If you would like to know more about Celtic spirituality and Ireland's heritage than we could possibly squeeze into this book, you might enjoy some of the following recommended resources.

Books

Of course, we would be remiss if we did not mention Steve Rabey's own reader-friendly survey, *In the House of Memory: Ancient Celtic Wisdom for Everyday Life* (Dutton/Plume), which explores thirteen key principles of Celtic spirituality. Reading this book will help you understand some of the pagan and Christian principles that led to the creation of many of the sites in this book.

Ancient Ireland: From Prehistory to the Middle Ages (Oxford) is a lavishly illustrated, oversized book that is well worth its $50 cost. With stunning photos by Jacqueline O'Brien and an authoritative text by Peter Harbison, the preeminent writer in this field, this is an excellent introduction to nearly two hundred major Irish monuments and sites. If you want to see everything but know you won't be able to, the book can help you plan a practical itinerary.

Harbison's *Guide to National and Historic Monuments of Ireland* (Gill and Macmillan) is a shorter book containing brief descriptions of more sites, along with maps and a nice introduction. His *Pre-Christian Ireland* (Thames and Hudson) is an acclaimed overview of Ireland's prehistoric people. Also helpful is Oxford's recently published *The Encyclopedia of Ireland* by Ciaran Brady.

Thomas Cahill's eloquent bestseller *How the Irish Saved Civilization* (Anchor/Doubleday) is a fascinating, bestselling introduction to Ireland's amazing monks and scholars. Edward Sellner's *Wisdom of the Celtic Saints* (Ave Maria Press) and Uinseann O'Maidin's *The Celtic Monk* (Cistercian Publications) provide additional details.

Nora Chadwick's *The Celts* (Penguin) covers the facts of ancient history, while Kenneth Hurlstone Jackson's *A Celtic Miscellany* (Penguin) features Irish, Welsh, and Scottish poetry and prose. Peter Berresford Ellis's *The Druids* (Eerdmans) explodes many myths about Ireland's pagan people.

Both Liam de Paor's *St. Patrick's World* (Four Courts Press) and Lisa Bitel's *Isle of the Saints* (Cork University Press) explore Celtic Christianity. Esther deWaal's *The Celtic Way of Prayer* (Doubleday) reveals the contemplative dimensions of Celtic Christian spirituality. *Celtic Christian Spirituality: An Anthology of Medieval and Modern Sources* (edited by Oliver Davies and Fiona Bowie and published by Continuum) is a fine collection which gathers together many interesting works. And Stephen Lawhead's sprawling novel *Byzantium* (Harper/Zondervan) uses a wealth of historical facts as the backdrop for a thrilling ride through long-ago times. Lawhead has also written other Celtic-flavored novels.

Information on specific saints can be found in these volumes: Patrick's two written works are reprinted and introduced in *Saint Patrick,* one of a series of small books on Celtic saints published by Scottish publisher Floris Books. Adoman of Iona's *Life of St. Columba* (Penguin) is a fascinating read. We like John J. O'Meara's excellent translation of *The Voyage of Saint Brendan* (Smythe), but other translations are available.

The following books cover specific sites or types of sites:

- *The Boyne: A Valley of Kings* (by Boylan; published by O'Brien)
- *The Dublin Literary Pub Crawl* (Costello; Farmar)
- *A Guide to Britain's Pagan Heritage* (Clarke; Hale)
- *Music Lover's Guide to Great Britain & Ireland* (Bianchi and Gusoff; Passport)
- *The Holy Wells of Ireland* (Logan; Colin Smythe)
- *The Stone Circles of Britain, Ireland and Brittany* (Burl; Yale University Press)
- *Irish Churches and Monasteries: An Historical & Architectural Guide* (O'Reilly; The Collins Press)
- *Glendalough: A Celtic Pilgrimage* (Rodgers and Losack; Morehouse)
- *An Iona Anthology* (McNeill; The New Iona Press)
- *St. Patrick's Purgatory* (Picard and Pontfarcy; Four Courts Press), and *Lough Derg: St. Patrick's Purgatory* (McGuinness; Columba)
- *Inishmurray: Ancient Monastic Island* (Heraughty; O'Brien)
- *Ireland's Islands* (Somerville-Large; Gill & Macmillan)
- *The Skellig Story* (Lavelle; O'Brien) explores the history of this island, while *Sundancing: A Medieval Vision* (Moorehouse; Weidenfeld and Nicolson) takes a fictional approach.

Many of these books are published in Ireland, and not all of them are readily available in North America. If you can't find them, contact the American distributor Irish Books and Media (telephone: 612-871-3505; fax: 612-871-3358; Web site: www.irishbook.com). If that doesn't work, try Kenny's Bookshop and Art Gallery in Galway, Ireland, which has one of the world's most extensive collections of Irish-related books, and ships to many loyal North American consumers (e-mail: queries@kennys.ie; telephone 353-91-562-739).

Music

The easiest way to start your Celtic music collection is by sending $5 to Maggie's Music, P.O. Box 4144, Annapolis, MD 21403 (telephone: 410-268-3394) for a sampler CD featuring the label's artists. Rego Irish Records and Tapes is an American distributor that offers hundreds of Irish recordings and videos (call 800-854-3746 for a catalog). The Narada label's Celtic Odyssey and Celtic Legacy are also nice samplers (414-961-8350). And Green Linnet's 1996 Twentieth Anniversary Collection is a diverse two-CD set (203-730-0333). The bimonthly magazine *Dirty Linen* devotes significant space to Celtic artists and music (410-583-7973).

Movies and Videos

We enjoy renting videos of Irish-themed films, and in recent years there have been plenty to choose from. Some of our favorites are *Waking Ned Devine, The Secret of Roan Inish, American Women, Dancing at Lughnasa, Into the West, Agnes Brown, Angela's Ashes, Ryan's Daughter, The Field, Some Mother's Son, The Boxer, In the Name of the Father, My Left Foot, Man of Aran, The Quiet Man, The Commitments, This Is My Father,* and *Darby O'Gill and the Little People.*

Anglican Canon Martin Shaw does an excellent job of explaining Celtic Christianity as he visits some of the Celts' major monastic sites in the two-volume video *Island Soldiers: The History of the Celtic Saints* (800-257-5126).

In addition, the Irish Tourist Board is an excellent source of updated information, publications, maps, and other material (call 800-223-6470).

Talks and Tours

The authors are available for lectures, presentations, and slide shows about the sites and subjects discussed in this book.

The authors also lead annual guided tours of Ireland's spiritual heritage. For information about the next "Celtic Journeys: Experiencing Ireland's Spiritual Legacy" tour, please give us your mailing address and we will send you a brochure. (Telephone: 719-386-6900; e-mail: loisrabey3@earthlink.net.)

Acknowledgments

Steve and Lois would like to thank the following people:

Our agent, Giles Anderson, who shared our excitement for this project from the beginning and made it possible for us to do it; Ann LaFarge and Margaret Wolf at Kensington Publishing, who made everything ship-shape; Paul Filidis, for helping us to create the maps in the book; and the innumerable kind, generous, and intriguing people in Ireland who have made our many visits there memorable and often moving.

INDEX

Abbeys, 107 (map), 118–20. *See also specific abbeys*
Accommodations. *See also specific accommodations and destinations*
  tips on, 152
Adoman, 131, 214
Aenghus, King, 29
Aengus, 108
Airlines, 142–43
Airports, 141–42
  exchanging money at, 148
Al's Italian Restaurant, 173
Amairgin, 40–41
Ancient tombs, 3–15, 5 (map). *See also specific tombs*
An Crugan, 158
An Da Chich Danann, 92
Angela's Ashes (McCourt), 43
  tour, in Limerick, 194
Anglesey, 103
Annadown, 130
Anu (goddess), 92
Apparition Chapel (Knock), 135
Aran Fisherman, 159
Aran Heritage Center, 160
Aran Islands, 42–43, 156–60
  accommodations, 158–59
  restaurants, 159
  shopping, 159–60
  traveling to, 156–57
Aran Islands (Synge), 44
Ardfert, 130
Ardilaun House, 179
Ards Peninsula, 183
Armagh, 21 (map), 23–24, 160–61
Arthur, King, 94
Ash-Rowan Townhouse, 162
Athlone, 109, 161
Athlone Castle, 161
Augustinian movement, about, 119

Baggage restrictions, 143
Ballinskelligs, 79
Ballintober Abbey, 119
Baltinglass Abbey, 119
Baltinglass Burial Mound, 61
Basilica of Our Lady (Knock), 129 (map), 135–36, 193
Beckett, Samuel, 40
Bed & breakfasts (B&Bs), 150, 152. *See also specific lodgings and destinations*
Belfast, 161–62
Belfast International Airport, 142
Belleek china, 146, 177
Beltane, 22
Berchan, Saint, 99
Bernard, Saint, 118
Bewley's Cafe, 173–74
Bistro Bianconi, 199
Blarney (town), 43 (map), 163
Blarney Castle, 41, 42, 163
Blarney Stone, 42, 163
Blarney Woolen Mills, 163
Blue Haven, 190
Boa Island (Lough Erne), 88, 194
Boat travel. *See* Ferries
Book of Kells (Dublin), 34–37, 114, 130, 169
Book of the Dun Cow, 109
Boyle Abbey, 118
Boyne River, 96
Boyne Valley, 184–85
Brecan, Saint, 156
Brendan, Saint, 86, 99, 108, 125–28, 214
  site associated with, 130
Brennan, Leo, 48. *See also* Leo's Tavern
Brennan's Restaurant, 165
Brian Boru, 23, 30
Brigid, Saint, 98, 110–11, 196–97
Browneshill Dolmen, 5 (map), 13, 163
Bru Boru Heritage Center, 166

Bru na Boinne. *See* Newgrange
Burren, the, 13–14, 176
Burt, 183–84
Bus travel, 145–46

Caeanannus Mor. *See* Kells
Caedmon, 47–48
Cahirsiveen, 163–65
Carlow, 165, 207
Carnelly House, 177
Carraig Donn, 203
Car rentals, 144
Carrowbeg River, 201
Carrowkeel, 5 (map), 12, 198
Carrowmore, 5 (map), 10–12, *11*,
    165–66
Car travel, 144–45
Cashel (town), 29, 166. *See also* Rock of
    Cashel
Castlecove, 200
Catholicism (Catholics), 23–24. *See also*
    specific saints
Ceanthru Mor. *See* Carrowmore
Celtic crosses. *See* High crosses
Celtic deities. *See specific deities*
Celtic music, viii–ix, 46–49, 216
  books about, 215
  Dublin, 170, 174
    Celtic Note Irish Music Store, 170
    Musical Pub Crawl, 170
  Ennis, 176
  Gweedore: Leo's Tavern, 48–49, 184
  Westport: Matt Molloy's Pub, 48, 201
Celtic Note Irish Music Store (Dublin),
    170
Celtic revival, viii–ix
Celts, x–xi
  belief system, 91–92, 124
  books about, 213–16
  fortresses and, 63–73
  holy wells and, 96–99, 215
  kinship, 66–69, 72–73
  mythology, 40–41, 67, 94
  naming the land, 101–3
  wanderlust and, 123–37
Ceoltoiri Cualann, 48
Chieftans, the (band), 48, 201
Christianity, xiii, 17, 102–3, 105. *See also*
    Monasteries; Monasticism; *and*
    specific saints and sites
  pilgrimages and, 56–57
Ciaran, Saint, 108–9
Circle rituals, about, 26–27

Cistercian movement, about, 118–19
Claddagh Jewellers (Galway), 180
Claddagh rings, 180
Clannad (band), 48–49, 184
Clans, about, 66–68
Clarecastle, 177
Cleggan, 86, 185
Clew Bay, 167
Cliffs of Moher, 14, 176
Clonakilty, 168
Clonfert Cathedral, 129 (map), 130
Clonmacnois, 107 (map), *117*, 166–67
Columba, Saint, 37, 53, 86, 89, 102,
    130–32, 186
  books about, 214
  Exhibition, 187
Columban, Saint, 133–35
Columba's Bay, 131
Columcille, Saint. *See* Columba, Saint
Conall, Saint, 99
Confessions (St. Patrick), 18–20
Cong Abbey, 119
Conyngham Arms Hotel, 184
Coole Park, 44
Court tombs, about, 13
Creevykeel, 13, 198
Cregmount House, 158
Croagh Patrick, 21 (map), 24–27, *25*,
    167, 201
Cromwell's Barracks, 86
Crowley, Aleister, 45
Crystal. *See specific makers*
CuChulain, 40
Currency and exchange, 147–48
Customs regulations, 146

Dagda, 47, 72
Danau, xii
Danube River, xii, 96, 101
Derrybawn House, 182
Devenish Island (Lough Erne), 88, 194
Dingle (town), 167–68
Dingle Peninsula, 167–68, 191
Dingle's Restaurant, 192
Dining. *See also specific restaurants and*
    destinations
  tips on, 152–53
Dolmen tombs, about, 11–14
Donegal china, 177
Doocaher, 66
Doon Farvagh, 66
Doon Fort, 70
Doon Lough, 70

Down Cathedral, 30–31
Down County Museum, 168
Downpatrick, 21 (map), 30–31, 168
Dowth, 10, 195–96
Doyle's Seafood Bar and Town House, 168
Drombeg, 97
Drombeg Stone Circle, 93 (map), *97*, 100, 168
Drumcliffe, 44
Drumsill Hotel, 161
Dublin, 21 (map), 42 (map), 169–75
    accommodations, 171–72
    arriving in, 171
    Celtic music, 170, 174
    excursions from, 175, 205–10
    information, 174
    itineraries, 205–10, 206 (map), 208 (map)
    pubs, 48, 174
        walking tours, 39, 170
    restaurants, 172–74
    services and amenities, 174
    shopping, 174
    sightseeing, 30, 34–37, 169–71
    walking tours, organized, 39–40, 170
Dublin Writers Museum, 40, 169
Dun Aengus, 64, 65 (map), 66, 156
Dun Aillinne, 93 (map), 96
Dun Aonghasa Seafood Restaurant and Bar, 159
Dunbeg Fort, *62*, 65 (map), 68–70, 167
Dun Conor, 66
Dungallan House Hotel, 188
Dun Moher, 66
Dun Onaght, 66
Duty-free shopping, 146, 151
Dysart Gallen, 76
Dysert O'Dea, 75, 77 (map), 176
Dysert Tola, 76

Enda, Saint, 86–87, 108–9, 126, 156
Ennis, 176–78
Ennis Friary, 176
Entry requirements, 147
Erc, Saint, 22
Eternal Youth, Well of (Iona), 131
Europe Hotel, 192

Farmhouse holidays, 153
Ferries
    Aran Islands, 157
    Ennis, 176–77

Inishbofin, 185
Inishmurray, 185
Iona, 186–87
    Scattery Island, 198
    Skellig Michael, 198
    Tory Island, 201
    Valentia Island, 164
Fethard, 119
Finan, Saint, 78, 86, 108
Fionnphort, 186–87
Fortresses, 63–73, 65 (map). *See also specific fortresses*
Fossa, 192
Francis, Saint, 119–20, 135
Fursey, Saint, 99

Gaby's Seafood, 192
Gall, Saint, 134
Gallarus Oratory, 107 (map), 120, 167
Galway (city), 178–81
    accommodations, 179
    ferries, 157
    information, 181
    restaurants, 179–80
    shopping, 180
    sightseeing, 178
Galway Irish Crystal Heritage Centre, 180
Glendalough, *50*, 51, 52 (map), 53–61, *57*, 181–83, 207
    accommodations near, 181–82
    books about, 215
    restaurants near, 182
    shopping near, 183
    visitor center, 181
Glendalough (town), 181–83
Glendalough Hotel, 182
Glendalough Woollen Mills, 183
Glenealo River, 59, 60
Gort, 44, 200
Gortahork, 201
Grafton Plaza, 171
Great Southern Hotel, 179
Grey Abbey, 107 (map), 119, 183
Grey Door, 173
Grianan Aileach Fort, 65 (map), 72, 183–84
Guided tours, of Ireland, 217
Gweedore, 42 (map), 48–49, 184

Hargagon's Pub, 199
Heaney, Seamus, 40

Heritage Cards, 151
High crosses, 106, 109–10, 114–15,
    194–95
Hill forts, about, 70–71
Hill of Slane, *16*, 21 (map), 22–23, 95,
    184, 207
Hill of Tara, 22, 92, 93 (map), 94–96,
    184–85, 207
Holywell, 97–98
Holy wells, about, 96–99, 215
Horse races, in Listowel, 194
Hotel Europe, 192
Hotels. *See also specific hotels and
    destinations*
    tips on, 152

Illuminated manuscripts, 33–38,
    130–31. *See also* Book of Kells
Information sources, 153–54, 213–16.
    See also Web sites; *and specific
    destinations*
Inishbofin, 77 (map), 86, 185
Inishdadroum, 130
Inisheer, 156–57
Inishmaan, 156–57
Inishmore, 42 (map), 63–64, 86, *90*,
    93 (map), 98–99, 107 (map),
    108, 156–60
    accommodations, 158–59
    restaurants, 159
    traveling to, 156–57
Inishmurray, 13, 77 (map), 84–85, 185,
    215
Inishowen Peninsula, 183–84
Iona, 37, *122*, 131–33, 186–89
    accommodations, 187–88
    books about, 215
    restaurants, 188
    shopping, 188–89
    traveling to, 186–87
Iona Abbey, 131–32, 187–88
Iona Community, 131–32, 187–88
Irish lace, in Kenmare, 190
Irish Rail, 146
Irish Tourist Board, 153, 216
Island monasteries, 75–89, 77 (map). *See
    also specific islands*
    traveling to. *See* Ferries
Itineraries, suggested, 205–11

Jarlath, Saint, 108
Jerpoint Abbey, 119

Joyce, James, 39
    Cultural Center (Dublin), 39–40, 169
Jury's Christchurch Inn, 172

K. C. Blakes Brasserie, 180
Kells (town), 42 (map), 115–16, 190, 207
Kells monastery, 37–38, 115–16, 190
Kenmare, 190–91
Kenmare Stone Circle, 93 (map), 191
Kenny's Bookshop & Art Gallery, *45*, 178
Kerry, Ring of, 164, 191, 200
Kevin, Saint, 51, 53–61. *See also*
    Glendalough
Kevin's Rule, 55
Kieran, Saint, 59
Kilbeggan, 103
Kilcolman, 103
Kilcullen, 103
Kildare, 107 (map), 111, 196–97, 207
Kilfithmone, 103
Killarney, 191–93
    accommodations, 192
    restaurants, 192–93
    sightseeing, 191
Killarney Park Hotel, 192
Killimer, 177
Kilmacduagh, 118
Kilmurvey House, 158–59
Kilronan, 157–60
Kilrush, 198
Kinsale, 189–90
Knitwear (woolens, sweaters)
    Aran sweaters, 159–60
    Blarney Woolen Mills, 163
    in Ennis, 178
    Glendalough Woollen Mills, 183
    Quills Woolen Market (Kenmare), 190
    in Westport, 203
Knochnarea, 13
Knock, 129 (map), *134*, 135–36, 193
Knockaderry, 102
Knockatober, 102
Knocknadrooa, 102
Knowth, 10, 195–96
Kylemore Abbey, 107 (map), 120–21, 193

Lace, in Kenmare, 190
Laragh, 58, 60, 181, 182
La Stampa, 173
Leo's Tavern, 48–49, 184
Lighthouse, the (Kinsale), 189
Limerick (town), 42 (map), 43, 193–94

Liscannor, 98
Listowel, 42 (map), 44, 194
Literature, 33–38, 40–41, 43–46. *See also*
    specific writers
    Dublin
        Literary Pub Crawl, 39, 170, 215
        Writers Museum, 40, 169
    festival, in Listowel, 44, 194
    sites associated with, 42 (map)
Live music. *See* Celtic music; Music
Llanfairpwllgwyngyllgogerychwyrndro-
    bwllllantysiliogogogoch, 103
Lodging. *See also specific lodgings and*
    destinations
    tips on, 152
Londonderry, 72
Lough Derg, 27–29, 197
Lough Erne, Lower, 77 (map), 88, 194
Lough Gill, 201
Lough Gur necropolis, 14
Lower Lough Erne, 77 (map), 88, 194
Lughnasa, 26

McCartney, Paul, 99
McCausland Hotel, 162
McCourt, Frank, 42, 193–94
McKennitt, Loreena, 81
Maeldune, Saint, 137
Mahee Island (Strangford Lough), 87, 195
Malachy, Saint, 106, 118–19
Manuscripts. *See* Book of Kells;
    Illuminated manuscripts
Maps, 145
Matthew's Gospel, 123–24
Matt Molloy's Pub, 48, 201
Medhbh, 11
Medications, 150
Megalithic tombs, 3–15, 5 (map). *See*
    also specific tombs
Mellifont Abbey, 106, 107 (map),
    118–19, 205
Mike Maguire's Gift Shoppe, 185, 207
Mochaoi, Saint, 87
Molaise, Saint, 84, 88
Monasterboice, *104*, 107 (map), 114–15,
    194–95, 205
Monasteries, 56, 76, 78, 105–21,
    107 (map). *See also specific*
    monasteries
    books about, 215
    illuminated manuscripts and, 33–38,
        130–31

island, 75–89, 77 (map)
soul friendship and, 112–13
Monasticism, 75–89, 108–10
Money, 147–48
Monoliths, about, 99–101
Mount Brandon, 130
Mount Eagle, 68
Mount Melleray Abbey, 83
Muiredach's Cross, 115
Mull, 132, 186
    ferries, 186–87
Mullaghmore, 84
Mullingar, 98
Music, 46–49. *See also* Celtic music

Naran, 70
National Park, Wicklow Mountains, 61,
    181, 207
Navan Centre, 160
Navan Fort, 93 (map), 95–96, 160
Nendrum Monastery, 77 (map), 87, 195
Newgrange, 2, 3–4, 5 (map), 6–10,
    195–96, 205
Northern Ireland. *See also specific*
    destinations
    currency, 147
    information, 153
    itineraries, suggested, 210
    traveling to, 142, 144, 145
Number 31 (Dublin), 172

Oban, 188
    ferries, 186–87
Ogmios (god), 40
Olde Railway Hotel, 202
Old Ground (Ennis), 177
O'Maidin, Uinseann, 55, 83–84, 112
O'Neill's the Point, 165
Organized tours, of Ireland, 217
Ostan Gweedore Hotel, 184

Paganism, xi–xii, xiii, 17, 91–92, 102
Paps of Anu, 92, 93 (map)
Parke's Castle, 44
Park House Hotel, 179
Park Room Restaurant, 179
Passage tombs, about, 10, 11
Passports, 147
Patrick, Saint, xiii, 17–31, 95, 102, 108,
    124
    biographical sketch of, 18–20
    books about, 214, 215

Patrick, Saint *(cont.)*
Cathedrals
Armagh, 23–24, 160–61, 197
Dublin, 30, 170–71, 197
Croagh Patrick, 219 (map), 24–27, *25*,
167, 201–2
Heritage Center (Downpatrick), 31,
168
Purgatory (Lough Derg), 21 (map),
27–29, 198
Rock of Cashel, 21 (map), 29–30, 166,
196–97
sites associated with, 21 (map), 22–31,
160–61, 167, 168, 184, 197
Pettigo, 197
Phone calls, 148–49
Pilgrimages, about, 56–57
Piper's Stones, 60–61, 93 (map), 101, 196
Portmagee, 198
Post offices, 148
Pottery, on Iona, 188–89
Poulnabrone Dolmen, 5 (map), 13–14,
176
Pound, Irish, 147–48
Priest's House (Glendalough), 59
Proleek Dolmen, 14
Pubs, 38–39. *See also specific destinations*
dining in, 153
Dublin Pub Crawl, 39, 170, 215

Quay Cottage (Westport), 202
Quills Woolen Market, 190

Rathdrum, 181, 182
Red Hill, 102
Reefert Church, 59
Reek Sunday, 26
Renard Point, 165
Restaurants. *See also specific restaurants
and destinations*
tips on, 152–53
Ring of Kerry, 191, 200
Rock of Cashel, 21 (map), 29–30, 166,
196
Rosaveel, 157
Rosses, the, 46
Rosses Point, 185
Round towers, about, 115–18
Royal Hotel (Killarney), 192
Royal Tara China Visitor Centre, 180
Rule of Ailbe, 83–84
Rule of Carthage, 113

Rule of Cormac Mac Ciolionain, 112
Rule of the Grey Monks, 112

Sacred stones. *See* Stone circles
Sacred wells, about, 96–99, 215
St. Brigid's Cathedral, 111, 196–97
St. Brigid's Monastery, 111, 196–97
Saint Columba Exhibition, 186
St. Columba Hotel, 187
St. Enda's Monastery, 86, *87*, 108–9, 156
St. Kevin's Bed, 60
St. Kevin's Cell, 59
St. Kevin's Church, 58
St. Kevin's Cross, 58
St. Kieran's Church, 59
St. Patrick Heritage Center, 31, 168
"St. Patrick's Breastplate," 27
St. Patrick's Cathedral (Dublin), 30,
170–71, 197
St. Patrick's Catholic Cathedral
(Armagh), 23–24, 160–61, 197
St. Patrick's Protestant Cathedral
(Armagh), 23, 160–61, 197
St. Patrick's Purgatory, 21 (map), 27–29,
197
St. Patrick's Rock. *See* Rock of Cashel
St. Patrick's Well, 31, 98
Scattery Island, 88, 198
Scott, Walter, 60, 132
Scriptoriums, about, 37–38
Senan, Saint, 88
Shannon River, 88, 109, 198
Sheila's (Killarney), 192
Shopping. *See also specific destinations
and items*
duty-free, 146, 151
packing tips, 150
tips for, 151
VAT, 146
Skellig Heritage Centre, 80, 164
Skellig Lighthouse, 164
Skellig Michael, *74*, 77 (map), 78–81,
164, 198
books about, 215–16
Slane (town), 184, 207. *See also* Hill of
Slane
Sligo (town), 198–200
Sligo Park Hotel, 199
Staigue Fort, 65 (map), 71–72, *71*, 200
Station Island (Lough Derg), 27–29, 197
Stone circles, 99–101, 215. *See also
specific circles*

Stonehenge, 4, 6, 100
Strangford Lough, 87, 195
Sweaters. *See* Knitwear
Swift, Jonathan, 30, 39
Synge, John Millington, 43–44

Tara. *See* Hill of Tara
Tarbert, 176–77
Taxes, VAT, 146
Teach Dolmain, 165
Teac Nan Paidi, 159
Teampall an Cheathrair Alainn, 99
Telephones, 148–49
Temple-na-Skellig, 60
Thoor Ballylee, 42 (map), 44, 200
Thornton's, 172
Timoleague Abbey, 107 (map), 119–20, 200
Tipperary (town), 166
Titanic, 162
Tobernalt Well, 93 (map), 98, 201
Tola, Saint, 75, 176
Tombs. *See* Megalithic tombs
Tory Island, 77 (map), 89, 201
Tourist information. *See* Information sources
Train travel, 145–46
Travel agents, 143
Traveler's checks, 148
Traveling
    to Ireland, xiv
    by air, 141–43
    within Ireland. *See also* Ferries
    by car, 144–45
    by train and bus, 145–46
Travel Web sites, 143
Tribes, about, 66–68
Trinity College (Dublin), 39, 98, 169.
    See also Book of Kells
Twelve Bens, 120

Valentia Island, 165, 198
VAT (value-added tax), 146
Virgin Mary, in Knock, 135–36, 193
Visas, 147
Visitor information. *See* Information sources
Voyage of Saint Brendan, 127–28, 214

Waterford crystal, 146, 177
Web sites, 153
    travel, 143
Wedge tombs, about, 13
Wells, about, 96–99, 215
Westbury, the, 171
West Cross (Monasterboice), 114–15, 194–95
West Ireland, itineraries for, 210, 211 (map)
Westport, 42 (map), 48, 167, 201–3
Whitby monastery, 48
White Island (Lough Erne), 88, 194
White Martyrdom, 124–25
Wicklow Heather (Laragh), 182
Wicklow Mountains, 53, 61
Wicklow Mountains National Park, 61, 181, 207
Wicklow Way, 60
Wilde, Oscar, 39
Winefride, Saint, 97–98
Winter Solstice, at Newgrange, 6, 9
Woolens. *See* Knitwear
Wordsworth, William, 132–33
Writers Museum, Dublin, 40, 169

Yeats, William Butler, 40, 43, 44–46, 198
Thoor Ballylee, 44, 200

About the Authors

Steve and Lois Rabey's regular visits to Ireland have only deepened their love for this amazing island. Together and individually they have written nearly twenty books and hundreds of articles. Steve's work has appeared in the *New York Times*, *New Age*, and *Christianity Today*. The couple leads annual Celtic Journeys tours exploring Ireland's spiritual legacy.